ISBN 978-0-260-52016-6
PIBN 10953580

This book is a reproduction of an important historical work. Forgotten Books uses
state-of-the-art technology to digitally reconstruct the work, preserving the original format
whilst repairing imperfections present in the aged copy. In rare cases, an imperfection in
the original, such as a blemish or missing page, may be replicated in our edition. We do,
however, repair the vast majority of imperfections successfully; any imperfections that
remain are intentionally left to preserve the state of such historical works.

For support please visit www.forgottenbooks.com

Document

lects current scientific knowledge,

FOREIGN AGRICULTURE CIRCULAR

U.S. DEPARTMENT OF AGRICULTURE
Foreign Agricultural Service   Washington D.C.

GRAIN
FG 1-68
March 1968

EXPORTS OF U.S. COARSE GRAIN

PRODUCTS INCREASE 16 PERCENT

Exports of all coarse grain products of 573,000 metric tons during
1966-67 exceeded the previous year's total of 494,000 tons by 16
percent. The comparable export totals for prior years, back to 1959-60,
have varied between 473,000 and 569,000 tons.

Coarse grain exports of 20.8 million tons were 18 percent below the
record shipments of 25.9 million tons exported during 1965-66. Even
so, 1966-67 exports were above any other prior years.

Corn products - Total corn products exports consisting of cornmeal,
hominy and grits, and cornstarch totaled 496,000 tons--an increase of
15 percent over the 430,000 tons shipped during 1965-66.

Cornmeal shipments totaled 415,000 tons and accounted for 84 percent
of all corn products. About 259,000 tons of this amount were donated
under government programs for relief. The largest recipients of relief
shipments were the Dominican Republic, Brazil, India, Morocco, and Senegal.
Cash sales totaled 156,000 tons compared with 65,000 tons last year. The
largest cash markets were Canada and the Republic of South Africa.

Exports of hominy and grits totaled 32,000 tons compared with 39,000 last
year. The decrease was caused mostly by smaller shipments to Venezuela
and Japan. This was partially offset by increased shipments to Canada.

COARSE GRAINS (grain equivalent): U.S. exports by country of destination, fiscal year 1966-67

Destination	Corn except seed	Corn seed except sweet	Corn for relief	Corn Meal	Hominy and grits	Corn starch	Corn meal for relief	Total
	Metric tons	Metric tons	Metric tons	Metric tons	Metric tons	Metric tons	Metric tons	Metric tons
North and Central America and Caribbean:								
Canada	1/ 484,825	2,604	680	45,217	21,809	13,787	40	568,962
Mexico	10,189	1,173	--	47	1,607	1,246	--	14,262
British Honduras	295	16	5	--	--	1	--	317
Costa Rica	51	4	810	--	--	1,402	494	2,761
El Salvador	125	--	--	383	--	320	3,011	3,839
Guatemala	101	--	--	--	--	100	2,189	2,390
Honduras	219	--	--	--	560	2,217	420	3,416
Nicaragua	56	22	1,826	--	--	29	417	2,350
Panama	358	15	--	29	--	3,903	754	5,059
Bahamas	3,463	7	--	275	2,469	43	--	6,257
Barbados	19	--	--	537	--	--	--	556
Bermuda	505	4	--	9	--	49	--	567
Dominican Republic	5,151	--	--	1,043	--	252	10,338	16,784
French West Indies	73	--	--	56	--	--	351	480
Haiti	4	9	82	--	--	111	4,220	4,426
Jamaica	34,713	224	--	749	--	1,405	1,911	39,002
Leeward and Windward Islands	883	--	--	485	--	1	2,789	4,158
Netherlands Antilles	1,300	14	--	6,418	--	10	52	7,794
Trinidad and Tobago	34,021	--	--	180	--	84	78	34,363
Total	576,351	4,092	3,403	55,428	26,445	24,960	27,064	717,743
South America:								
Argentina	--	74	--	--	--	--	--	74
Bolivia	29	--	51	--	--	13	2,135	2,228
Brazil	6,493	--	--	13,829	--	133	14,687	35,142
Chile	25,948	52	--	35	--	1,961	1,276	29,272
Colombia	539	20	580	--	--	8	9,646	10,793
Ecuador	86	2	--	177	--	4,961	3,947	9,173
Guyana	1,970	--	--	160	64	--	166	2,360
Paraguay	--	--	--	--	--	--	994	994
Peru	2,073	194	--	3,273	--	62	4,521	10,123
Surinam	218	1	--	62	--	89	--	370
Uruguay	--	1	--	--	--	--	1,254	1,255
Venezuela	1,173	27	--	23	1,385	596	9,337	12,541
Total	38,529	371	631	17,559	1,449	7,823	47,963	114,325
Western Europe:								
EEC:								
Belgium and Luxembourg	776,253	112	--	89	--	464	--	776,918
France	53,549	267	--	72	--	514	--	54,402
Germany, West	997,566	2,430	2,032	48	--	991	--	1,003,067
Italy	999,466	852	--	--	--	492	--	1,000,810
Netherlands	2,453,937	165	--	466	1,418	271	--	2,456,257
EEC sub-total	5,280,771	3,826	2,032	675	1,418	2,732	--	5,291,454
Austria	212	17	--	--	--	14	--	243
Cyprus	1,037	--	--	--	--	--	--	1,037
Denmark	14,134	--	--	218	--	17	--	14,369
Finland	4,199	--	--	7	--	1,134	22	5,362
Greece	136,153	--	--	16	--	19	910	137,098
Iceland	5,191	--	--	--	--	--	--	5,191
Ireland	42,019	--	--	--	960	75	--	43,054
Malta	--	--	--	--	--	--	57	57
Norway	58,267	--	--	--	263	1,288	--	59,818
Portugal	77,800	76	--	--	--	--	7,709	85,585
Spain	915,285	763	--	--	--	26	2,317	918,391
Sweden	2,960	10	--	217	774	212	--	4,173
Switzerland	67,329	7	--	--	--	175	--	67,511
United Kingdom	1,902,315	8	--	1,249	13	6,777	--	1,910,362
Total	8,507,672	4,707	2,032	2,382	3,428	12,469	11,015	8,543,705
Eastern Europe:								
Bulgaria	--	--	--	--	--	--	--	--
Czechoslovakia	8,000	20	--	--	--	--	--	8,020
Germany, East	229,552	--	--	--	--	--	--	229,552
Hungary	--	27	--	--	--	--	--	27
Poland	157,305	--	--	--	--	--	2,527	159,832
Yugoslavia	15,042	--	--	435	--	--	578	16,055
Total	409,899	47	--	435	--	--	3,105	413,486
Total all Europe	8,917,571	4,754	2,032	2,817	3,428	12,469	14,120	8,957,191

COARSE GRAINS (grain equivalent): U.S. exports by country of destination, fiscal year 1966-67

Oats	Oats and Products — Oatmeal: Oatmeal and groats, nec.	Oatmeal to be cooked	Total	Barley and Products: Barley	Malt	Total	Grain sorghums	Grand total all grains & products	Destination
Metric tons	Metric tons	Metric tons	Metric tons	Metric tons	Metric tons	Metric tons	Metric tons	Metric tons	
									North and Central America and Caribbean:
1/ 45	—	3	48	1/ —	1,769	1,769	40,984	611,763	Canada
3,768	4,958	—	8,726	1/ 36,068	753	36,821	25,239	85,042	Mexico
—	—	17	17	—	—	—	—	334	British Honduras
10	102	—	112	—	808	808	46	3,727	Costa Rica
6	—	2/	6	—	14	14	13	3,872	El Salvador
—	—	4	4	—	87	87	20	2,501	Guatemala
—	—	46	46	—	3,820	3,820	—	7,282	Honduras
—	1,586	16	1,602	—	298	298	183	4,433	Nicaragua
201	—	59	260	—	99	99	—	5,418	Panama
347	—	37	384	—	4	4	11	6,656	Bahamas
—	—	—	—	—	269	269	91	916	Barbados
2	—	3	5	—	—	—	—	572	Bermuda
20	—	391	411	—	3,211	3,211	63	20,469	Dominican Republic
—	—	—	—	—	—	—	—	480	French West Indies
—	—	2	2	—	—	—	—	4,428	Haiti
424	—	23	447	—	1,753	1,753	5,992	47,194	Jamaica
4	—	2/	4	—	33	33	—	4,195	Leeward and Windward Islands
—	—	13	13	—	10	10	48	7,865	Netherlands Antilles
72	35	—	107	—	—	—	91	34,561	Trinidad and Tobago
4,899	6,681	614	12,194	36,068	12,928	48,996	72,781	851,714	Total
									South America:
—	—	—	—	—	—	—	745	819	Argentina
—	—	31	31	—	141	141	—	2,400	Bolivia
—	—	177	177	—	634	634	7,258	43,211	Brazil
—	—	96	96	2,700	—	2,700	—	32,068	Chile
34	1,879	249	2,162	—	7	7	29	12,991	Colombia
—	—	14	14	—	159	159	200	9,546	Ecuador
—	—	—	—	—	664	664	—	3,024	Guyana
—	—	—	—	—	—	—	—	994	Paraguay
—	—	84	84	—	936	936	8,441	19,584	Peru
—	28	30	58	—	—	—	—	428	Surinam
—	—	—	—	—	—	—	—	1,255	Uruguay
123	1,763	—	1,886	—	29,977	29,977	400	44,804	Venezuela
157	3,670	681	4,508	2,700	32,518	35,218	17,073	171,124	Total
									Western Europe:
									EEC:
30,923	—	—	30,923	21,365	8	21,373	516,902	1,346,116	Belgium and Luxembourg
—	—	—	—	—	—	—	568	54,970	France
80,512	—	—	80,512	115,611	—	115,611	153,176	1,352,366	Germany, West
37,698	—	2/	37,698	235,968	—	235,968	7,611	1,276,087	Italy
53,018	—	—	53,018	28,801	—	28,801	525,268	3,063,344	Netherlands
202,151	—	—	202,151	401,745	8	401,753	1,197,525	7,092,883	EEC sub-total
—	—	—	—	—	—	—	—	243	Austria
—	—	—	—	28,833	—	28,833	—	29,870	Cyprus
—	—	14	14	69,537	—	69,537	—	83,920	Denmark
—	—	—	—	—	—	—	—	5,362	Finland
—	—	—	—	—	—	—	—	137,098	Greece
—	—	—	—	472	—	472	—	5,663	Iceland
—	—	—	—	10,129	—	10,129	5,634	58,817	Ireland
—	—	—	—	—	—	—	2,523	2,580	Malta
—	—	1	1	—	—	—	91,758	151,576	Norway
—	—	—	—	15	—	15	43,372	128,958	Portugal
—	—	—	—	—	—	—	6,479	924,885	Spain
—	—	—	—	—	—	—	—	4,173	Sweden
19,860	—	—	19,860	—	—	—	2,043	89,414	Switzerland
—	976	1	977	—	56	56	52,286	1,963,681	United Kingdom
222,011	976	16	223,003	510,731	64	510,795	1,401,620	10,679,123	Total
									Eastern Europe:
—	—	—	—	—	—	—	350	350	Bulgaria
—	—	—	—	—	—	—	275,488	283,508	Czechoslovakia
—	—	—	—	14,227	—	14,227	60,598	304,377	Germany, East
—	—	—	—	—	—	—	39,332	39,359	Hungary
—	—	—	—	28,449	—	28,449	129,875	318,156	Poland
—	—	—	—	—	—	—	—	16,055	Yugoslavia
—	—	—	—	42,676	—	42,676	505,643	961,805	Total
222,011	976	16	223,003	553,407	64	553,471	1,907,263	11,640,928	Total all Europe

COARSE GRAINS (grain equivalent): U.S. exports by country of destination, fiscal year 1966-67

Destination	Corn except seed	Corn seed except sweet	Corn for relief	Corn Meal	Hominy and grits	Corn starch	Corn meal for relief	Total
	Metric tons	Metric tons	Metric tons	Metric tons	Metric tons	Metric tons	Metric tons	Metric tons
Africa:								
Algeria	---			--			2,263	2,263
British Africa	--	—	—	—	—	—	20	20
Burundi and Rwanda	184	—	23	—	—	—	262	469
Cameroon	370	—	—	—	—	—	13	383
Canary Islands	103,141	—	—	—	—	11	—	103,152
Central African Republic	--	—	--	—	—	—	—	--
Congo (Kinshasa)	228	—	563	106	—	—	6,881	7,778
Ethiopia	146	—	215	5	—	4	110	480
French Somaliland	—	—	—	—	—	—	68	68
Gambia	—	—	--	—	—	—	17	17
Ghana	9,442	—	268	—	—	3	4,480	14,193
Ivory Coast	5,755	—	—	—	—	—	1,090	6,845
Kenya	349	—	—	—	—	33	659	1,041
Liberia	94	—	—	371	—	60	979	1,504
Libya	125	8	—	—	—	3	--	136
Malagasy	--	—	—	—	—	--	177	177
Malawi	4	—	—	—	—	2	75	81
Mauritania	—	—	—	—	—	—	103	103
Mauritius	—	—	—	—	—	—	216	216
Morocco	5,520	—	—	796	—	—	27,390	33,706
Mozambique	—	—	—	11	—	1	—	12
Nigeria	303	—	—	12	—	74	2,869	3,258
Senegal	2,039	—	—	—	—	--	13,530	15,569
Seychelles	—	—	—	—	—	—	71	71
Sierra Leone	21	—	—	5	—	—	2,300	2,326
Somali Republic	—	—	—	—	—	—	2,159	2,159
South Africa, Republic of	5,452	29	—	24,340	—	52	5,122	34,995
Southern Africa, n.e.c.	—	—	—	567	—	—	1,032	1,599
Spanish Africa, n.e.c.	—	—	—	—	—	4	—	4
Sudan	—	—	—	--	—	3	154	157
Tanzania	1,470	—	—	—	—	—	5,588	7,058
Togo	120	—	—	136	—	—	682	938
Tunisia	35,579	—	—	—	—	—	2,476	38,055
Uganda	601	--	—	—	—	—	382	983
United Arab Republic	31,976	2	—	—	—	2	—	31,980
Western Africa, n.e.c.	6,652	—	—	—	—	—	3,774	10,426
Zambia	9	—	—	—	—	—	8,648	8,657
Total	209,580	39	1,069	26,349	—	252	93,590	330,879
Asia:								
Aden	333	—	—	—	—	—	58	391
Afghanistan	14,969	—	—	—	—	—	—	14,969
Arabian Peninsula States, n.e.c.	75	16	—	—	—	—	—	91
Bahrein	168	—	—	4	—	1	170	343
Burma	—	—	—	—	—	—	345	345
Cambodia	—	—	—	—	—	—	13	13
Ceylon	4,400	—	—	—	—	121	—	4,521
Hong Kong	5,355	—	—	14	—	107	731	6,207
India	109,012	2	—	1,118	—	6	48,257	158,395
Indonesia	687	—	4,666	—	—	24	958	6,335
Iran	301	31	—	4	—	23	513	872
Iraq	346	—	—	—	—	—	—	346
Israel	121,602	25	—	—	—	206	—	121,833
Japan	1,946,417	110	—	69	173	13	—	1,946,782
Jordan	28,482	—	—	722	—	—	533	29,737
Korea, Republic of	25,891	—	2,000	25,557	94	148	7,860	61,550
Kuwait	287	—	—	20	—	4	—	311
Laos	—	—	—	2,640	—	—	284	2,924
Lebanon	32,200	22	—	—	—	21	395	32,638
Malaysia	342	—	—	301	—	2	1,404	2,049
Macao	—	—	—	—	—	--	47	47
Nansei and Nanpo Islands	1,130	179	—	—	—	111	481	1,901
Pakistan	404,764	--	—	--	—	5	46	404,815
Philippines	45,164	13	221	1,966	286	1,345	7,734	56,729
Saudi Arabia	1,828	—	—	—	15	19	—	1,862
Singapore	435	—	—	—	—	--	863	1,298
Syria	40	—	—	—	—	—	2,370	2,410
Taiwan	2,875	31	—	—	—	17	—	2,923
Thailand	168	4	—	—	—	7	355	534
Turkey	—	—	—	—	—	—	208	208
Viet-nam, South	37,551	—	—	22,292	92	152	769	60,856
Total	2,784,822	433	6,887	54,707	660	2,332	74,394	2,924,235
Oceania:								
Australia	83	—	--	—	—	382	218	683
British Western Pacific Islands	--	—	—	—	—	—	849	849
French Pacific Islands	6	1	--	—	—	18	—	25
New Zealand	20	26	—	—	—	123	302	471
Trust Territory of Pacific Islands	7	2	—	8	—	16	116	149
Total	116	29	—	8	—	539	1,485	2,177
World Total	12,526,969	9,718	14,022	156,868	31,982	48,375	258,616	13,046,550
Equivalent, 1,000 bushels	493,160	383	552	6,176	1,259	1,904	10,181	513,615

1/ Adjusted to cover transhipments through Canadian ports which are included in data for countries of ultimate destination. 2/ Less than .5 metric tons.

COARSE GRAINS (grain equivalent): U.S. exports by country of destination, fiscal year 1966-67

Oats	Oats and Products			Barley and Products			Grain sorghums	Grand total all grains & products	Destination
	Oatmeal and groats, nec.	Oatmeal to be cooked	Total	Barley	Malt.	Total			
Metric tons	Metric tons	Metric tons	Metric tons	Metric tons	Metric tons	Metric tons	Metric tons	Metric tons	
									Africa:
5,258	—	6	5,264	9,397	—	9,397	—	16,924	Algeria
—	—	—	—	—	—	—	—	20	British West Africa
—	—	—	—	—	—	—	—	469	Burundi and Rwanda
—	—	—	—	—	—	—	—	383	Cameroon
—	—	—	—	—	—	—	2,666	105,818	Canary Islands
—	—	41	41	—	—	—	—	41	Central African Republic
—	—	—	—	—	4,936	4,936	180	12,894	Congo (Kinshasa)
—	—	3	3	—	—	—	1,318	1,801	Ethiopia
—	—	—	—	—	—	—	—	68	French Somaliland
—	—	—	—	—	—	—	—	17	Gambia
—	—	20	20	—	—	—	4,383	18,596	Ghana
—	—	—	—	—	—	—	100	6,945	Ivory Coast
—	—	15	15	—	—	—	602	1,643	Kenya
—	—	—	—	—	—	—	—	1,519	Liberia
—	—	—	—	9,553	—	9,553	—	9,689	Libya
—	—	3	3	—	—	—	—	180	Malagasy
—	—	5	5	—	—	—	—	86	Malawi
—	—	—	—	—	—	—	—	103	Mauritania
—	—	—	—	—	—	—	—	216	Mauritius
—	—	22	22	21,337	—	21,337	—	55,043	Morocco
—	—	—	—	—	—	—	—	34	Mozambique
—	—	—	—	—	—	—	500	3,758	Nigeria
—	—	—	—	—	—	—	40,904	56,473	Senegal
—	—	—	—	—	—	—	—	71	Seychelles
—	—	18	18	—	6	6	—	2,350	Sierra Leone
—	—	—	—	—	—	—	—	2,159	Somali Republic
—	—	—	—	—	—	—	3,610	38,605	South Africa, Republic of
—	—	—	—	—	—	—	—	1,599	Southern Africa, n.e.c.
—	—	—	—	—	—	—	—	4	Spanish Africa, n.e.c.
—	—	—	—	—	—	—	51,852	52,009	Sudan
—	—	—	—	—	—	—	849	7,907	Tanzania
—	—	—	—	—	—	—	—	938	Togo
2,148	—	—	2,148	76,051	—	76,051	1,539	117,793	Tunisia
—	—	—	—	—	—	—	—	983	Uganda
—	—	—	—	—	—	—	225	32,205	United Arab Republic'
—	—	—	—	—	—	—	29,205	39,631	Western Africa, n.e.c.
—	—	—	—	—	—	—	—	8,657	Zambia
7,406	—	133	7,539	116,338	4,942	121,280	137,933	597,631	Total
									Asia:
—	—	—	—	—	—	—	838	1,229	Aden
—	—	—	—	—	—	—	—	14,969	Afghanistan
—	—	—	—	—	—	—	1,372	1,463	Arabian Peninsula States
—	—	—	—	—	—	—	—	343	Bahrein
—	—	—	—	—	—	—	—	345	Burma
—	—	—	—	—	—	—	—	13	Cambodia
—	—	—	—	—	—	—	—	4,521	Ceylon
—	4	—	4	—	—	—	—	6,211	Hong Kong
—	—	1	1	—	—	—	2,169,996	2,328,392	India
—	—	—	—	—	—	—	—	6,335	Indonesia
—	—	—	—	—	—	—	—	872	Iran
—	—	—	—	—	—	—	—	346	Iraq
—	—	—	—	14,529	—	14,529	337,487	473,849	Israel
1,016	—	—	1,016	181,297	1,200	182,497	2,424,837	4,555,132	Japan
—	—	—	—	2,575	—	2,575	—	32,312	Jordan
—	—	1	1	—	2	2	—	61,553	Korea, Republic of
—	—	—	—	—	—	—	—	311	Kuwait
—	—	—	—	29,277	—	29,277	7,632	69,547	Lebanon
—	—	—	—	—	—	—	—	2,049	Malaysia
—	—	—	—	—	—	—	—	47	Macao
—	—	2	2	—	—	—	—	1,903	Nansei and Nanpo Islands
—	—	—	—	—	—	—	19,409	424,224	Pakistan
45	34	30	109	—	186	186	3,283	60,307	Philippines
—	—	10	10	—	—	—	—	1,872	Saudi Arabia
—	—	—	—	—	—	—	—	1,298	Singapore
10,249	—	—	10,249	—	—	—	240	12,899	Syria
—	—	—	—	—	—	—	—	2,923	Taiwan
—	5	—	5	—	15	15	44	598	Thailand
—	—	—	—	—	—	—	—	208	Turkey
—	—	12,565	12,565	—	—	—	—	73,421	Vietnam, South
11,310	43	12,609	23,962	227,678	1,403	229,081	4,965,138	8,142,416	Total
									Oceania:
—	—	4	4	—	—	—	—	687	Australia
—	—	—	—	—	—	—	—	849	British Western Pacific Islands
—	—	2	—	—	—	—	—	27	French Pacific Islands
—	—	2	2	—	—	—	—	471	New Zealand
—	—	—	—	—	—	—	—	151	Trust Territory of Pacific Islands
—	—	8	8	—	—	—	—	2,185	Total
245,783	11,370	14,061	271,214	936,191	51,855	988,046	7,100,188	21,405,998	World Total
16,923	783	969	18,685	42,998	2,382	45,380	279,519	—	Equivalent, 1,000 bushels

COARSE GRAINS (grain equivalent): U.S. exports by country Of destination, fiscal year 1965-66

Destination	Corn except seed	Corn seed except sweet	Corn for relief	Corn Meal	Hominy and grits	Corn starch	Corn meal for relief	Total
	Metric tons	Metric tons	Metric tons	Metric tons	Metric tons	Metric tons	Metric tons	Metric tons
North and Central America and Caribbean:								
Canada	1/ 546,894	3,096	1,047	28,548	17,900	14,824	326	612,635
Mexico	11,403	744	14	8	1,602	1,044	808	15,623
British Honduras	23	2	79	—	—	14	—	118
Costa Rica	312	14	571	—	—	1,113	—	2,010
El Salvador	1,604	19	—	1,715	'—	523	3,712	7,573
Guatemala	192	29	—	—	—	200	1,689	2,110
Honduras	416	3	2,036	133	'•78	1,491	1,525	5,674
Nicaragua	21	12	1,787	—	—	14	—	1,834
Panama	20,056	4	—	14	—	4,446	1,402	25,922
Bahamas	2,911	31	—	143	2,946	70	—	6,101
Barbados	184	—	—	540	—	—	—	724
Bermuda	231	3	—	9	—	41	—	284
Dominican Republic	24	8	—	460	920	212	17,062	18,686
French West Indies	576	—	—	36	—	194	267	1,073
Haiti	5	23	—	—	—	151	2,210	2,389
Jamaica	26,039	254	—	717	104	238	2,284	29,636
Leeward and Windward Islands	988	—	—	309	—	1	317	1,615
Netherlands Antilles	1,755	—	—	5,706	—	15	—	7,476
Trinidad and Tobago	16,730	6	—	196	127	62	29	17,150
Total	630,364	4,248	5,534	38,534	23,669	24,653	31,631	758,633
South America:								
Argentina	—	96	—	—	—	15	—	111
Bolivia	34	2	—	—	—	10	—	46
Brazil	5,000	—	—	3,982	—	354	12,538	21,874
Chile	25,429	41	—	331	—	697	2,626	29,124
Colombia	999	9	—	—	—	3	4,185	5,196
Ecuador	11	2/	—	—	—	4,777	2,052	6,840
Guyana	1,535	2	180	214	26	—	161	2,118
Paraguay	—	—	—	—	—	—	1,022	1,022
Peru	2,126	6	—	2,164	—	42	1,426	5,764
Surinam	853	—	—	58	—	340	—	1,251
Uruguay	—	4	—	—	—	—	856	860
Venezuela	57,224	—	—	28	6,397	953	6,790	71,392
Total	93,211	160	180	6,777	6,423	7,191	31,656	145,598
Western Europe:								
EEC:								
Belgium and Luxembourg	1,015,086	24	14	—	—	865	—	1,015,989
France	78,589	325	—	—	—	529	—	79,443
Germany, West	1,257,570	3,018	—	43	797	359	—	1,261,787
Italy	2,571,304	1,902	—	—	—	103	2,850	2,576,159
Netherlands	2,639,751	250	—	619	946	382	—	2,641,948
EEC sub-total	7,562,300	5,519	14	662	1,743	2,238	2,850	7,575,326
Austria	126,704	254	—	—	—	—	14	126,972
Cyprus	6,350	9	—	—	—	—	—	6,359
Denmark	9,937	7	—	119	350	35	—	10,448
Finland	10,222	10	—	44	—	1,416	—	11,692
Greece	309,202	—	—	—	—	4	846	310,052
Iceland	586	—	—	1,697	—	—	—	2,283
Ireland	126,242	—	—	—	—	30	—	126,272
Malta	2,040	—	—	4	—	—	—	2,044
Norway	106,271	2	—	—	437	2,203	—	108,913
Portugal	97,646	266	—	—	—	—	1,946	99,858
Spain	1,811,613	333	—	—	—	23	—	1,811,969
Sweden	2,937	6	—	—	762	438	—	4,143
Switzerland	67,461	—	—	—	—	1,309	—	68,770
Turkey	6,867	—	—	—	—	—	71	6,938
United Kingdom	2,369,175	93	—	1,176	403	13,438	—	2,384,285
Total	12,615,553	6,499	14	3,702	3,695	21,134	5,727	12,656,324
Eastern Europe:								
Bulgaria	—	—	—	—	—	—	—	—
Czechoslovakia	220,175	16	—	—	—	—	—	220,191
Germany, East	183,253	—	—	—	—	—	—	183,253
Hungary	5,080	5	—	—	—	—	—	5,085
Poland	—	—	—	—	—	—	1,956	1,956
U.S.S.R.	—	2/	—	—	—	—	—	2/
Yugoslavia	13,503	35	—	—	—	—	34	13,572
Total	422,011	56	—	—	—	—	1,990	424,057
Total all Europe	13,037,564	6,555	14	3,702	3,695	21,134	7,717	13,080,381

COARSE GRAINS (grain equivalent): U.S. exports by country of destination, fiscal year 1965-66

Oats	Oatmeal and groats, nec.	Oatmeal to be cooked	Total (Oats and Products)	Barley	Malt	Total (Barley and Products)	Grain sorghums	Grand total: all grains & products	Destination
Metric tons	Metric tons	Metric tons	Metric tons	Metric tons	Metric tons	Metric tons	Metric tons	Metric tons	
									North and Central America and Caribbean:
1/ 55	—	14	69	1/ —	651	651	4,867	698,222	Canada
11,553	6,184	3	17,740	61,117	1,982	63,099	55,857	152,319	Mexico
3	—	16	19	—	—	—	—	138	British Honduras
9	43	—	52	6	875	881	16	2,959	Costa Rica
—	126	13	139	—	19	19	54	7,646	El Salvador
—	—	49	49	100	78	178	62	2,489	Guatemala
—	1,880	8	1,888	—	4,066	4,066	177	9,966	Honduras
—	—	—	—	—	242	242	112	4,076	Nicaragua
64	—	56	120	—	1,015	1,015	—	27,057	Panama
319	—	44	363	—	16	16	17	6,497	Bahamas
—	—	2	2	—	163	163	385	1,272	Barbados
—	—	—	—	—	—	—	—	286	Bermuda
103	—	491	594	—	2,183	2,183	—	21,463	Dominican Republic
—	—	2	2	—	—	—	7	1,073	French West Indies
371	—	49	420	—	1,790	1,790	5,247	2,398	Haiti
—	—	1	1	—	34	34	—	37,093	Jamaica
—	—	3	3	—	31	31	15	1,650	Leeward and Windward Islands
—	—	—	—	—	—	—	—	7,525	Netherlands Antilles
109	—	1	110	—	—	—	4,344	21,604	Trinidad and Tobago
12,586	8,233	752	21,571	61,223	13,145	74,368	71,160	925,732	Total
									South America
—	—	—	—	—	7	7	1,065	1,176	Argentina
—	—	9	9	—	—	—	—	62	Bolivia
—	—	—	—	—	—	—	12,670	34,544	Brazil
—	—	1	1	—	—	—	—	29,125	Chile
34	—	—	34	50,952	2,117	53,069	960	59,259	Colombia
200	173	10	383	—	272	272	65	7,560	Ecuador
—	—	—	—	—	539	539	—	2,657	Guyana
—	—	27	27	—	—	—	47	1,069	Paraguay
—	—	—	—	—	1,045	1,045	1,090	7,926	Peru
—	—	13	13	—	—	—	—	1,264	Surinam
—	—	—	—	—	—	—	162	1,022	Uruguay
304	1,572	2	1,878	—	32,492	32,492	57	105,819	Venezuela
538	1,745	62	2,345	50,952	36,472	87,424	16,116	251,483	Total
									Western Europe:
									EEC:
43,163	—	—	43,163	39,171	—	39,171	752,551	1,850,874	Belgium and Luxembourg
620	—	—	620	—	—	—	9,720	89,783	France
137,383	—	—	137,383	417,318	—	417,318	294,184	2,110,672	Germany, West
90,164	—	1	90,165	301,341	—	301,341	7,452	2,975,117	Italy
209,599	—	—	209,599	106,024	—	106,024	908,809	3,866,380	Netherlands
480,929	—	1	480,930	863,854	—	863,854	1,972,716	10,892,826	EEC sub-total
3,500	—	—	3,500	—	—	—	6,419	136,891	Austria
—	—	—	—	—	—	—	—	6,359	Cyprus
759	—	—	759	127,453	—	127,453	213	138,873	Denmark
—	—	—	—	—	—	—	—	11,692	Finland
—	—	—	—	20,321	—	20,321	16,449	346,822	Greece
23	—	—	23	1,842	—	1,842	—	4,148	Iceland
—	—	—	—	2,926	—	2,926	53,131	182,329	Ireland
—	—	—	—	—	—	—	538	2,582	Malta
—	—	2/	—	10,749	—	10,749	70,024	189,686	Norway
—	—	—	—	—	—	—	33,723	133,581	Portugal
—	—	—	—	38,506	—	38,506	96,596	1,947,071	Spain
—	—	—	—	—	—	—	—	4,143	Sweden
24,651	—	—	24,651	7,721	—	7,721	17,545	118,687	Switzerland
—	—	—	—	—	—	—	—	6,938	Turkey
—	255	8	263	21,969	—	21,969	156,057	2,562,574	United Kingdom
509,862	255	9	510,126	1,095,341	—	1,095,341	2,423,411	16,685,202	Total
									Eastern Europe:
—	—	—	—	—	—	—	10,222	10,222	Bulgaria
—	—	—	—	47,498	—	47,498	383,071	650,760	Czechoslovakia
—	—	—	—	—	—	—	66,148	249,401	Germany, East
—	—	—	—	26,721	—	26,721	21,338	26,423	Hungary
—	—	—	—	—	—	—	—	28,677	Poland
—	—	—	—	—	—	—	—	2/	U.S.S.R.
—	—	—	—	—	—	—	—	13,572	Yugoslavia
—	—	—	—	74,219	—	74,219	480,779	979,055	Total
509,862	255	9	510,126	1,169,560	—	1,169,560	2,904,190	17,664,257	Total all Europe

COARSE GRAINS.(grain equivalent): U.S. exports by country of destination, fiscal year 1965-66

Destination	Corn except seed	Corn seed except sweet	Corn for relief	Corn Meal	Hominy and grits	Corn starch	Corn meal for relief	Total
	Metric tons	Metric tons	Metric tons	Metric tons	Metric tons	Metric tons	Metric tons	Metric tons
Africa:								
Algeria	—	—	17	—	—	—	—	17
Angola	214	—	—	—	—	45	—	259
Burundi and Rwanda	9	—	—	370	—	1	—	.380
Canary Islands	87,407	—	—	—	—	36	—	87,443
Congo (Kinshasa)	4	—	—	53	—	9	2,158	2,224
Ethiopia	294	—	—	19	—	—	—	313
French Somaliland	—	—	—	—	—	—	—	—
Ghana	2,287	—	182	—	—	—	1,423	3,892
Guinea	100	—	—	—	—	—	—	100
Ivory Coast	—	—	—	—	—	—	994	994
Kenya	180,912	2	—	4	—	14	1,957	182,889
Liberia	145	—	—	247	28	41	674	1,135
Libya	28	23	—	45	—	5	—	101
Malagasy Republic	—	—	—	—	—	—	3,734	3,734
Malawi	16	—	—	—	—	—	—	16
Morocco	32,931	—	—	—	—	—	10,311	43,242
Mozambique	471	—	—	6	—	—	89	566
Nigeria	220	—	—	57	—	20	1,458	1,755
Rhodesia	—	—	—	—	—	—	1,308	1,308
Senegal	6,018	—	—	15	—	—	8,960	14,993
Sierra Leone	60	—	—	123	—	—	2,134	2,317
Somali Republic	—	—	—	—	—	—	1,362	1,362
South Africa, Republic of	159,795	43	—	12,789	—	44	23	172,694
Spanish Africa, n.e.c.	—	—	—	—	—	3	—	3
Tanzania	11,079	—	—	—	—	—	10,425	21,504
Togo	—	—	—	1,362	—	—	565	1,927
Tunisia	14,169	—	270	—	—	—	3,647	18,086
Uganda	195	—	—	—	—	—	—	195
United Arab Republic	2,550	—	—	—	—	3	6,037	8,590
Western Africa, n.e.c.	1,032	—	—	24	—	—	1,209	2,265
Zambia	19	3	—	301	—	2	—	325
Total	499,355	71	469	15,415	28	223	58,468	574,629
Asia:								
Aden	121	—	—	—	—	—	—	121
Afghanistan	—	1	—	—	—	—	—	1
Arabian Peninsula States	129	22	—	—	—	221	—	372
Bahrein	101	—	—	—	—	3	—	104
Ceylon	—	—	—	—	—	98	—	98
Hong Kong	5,116	—	—	6	—	115	274	5,511
India	56,543	5	—	—	—	3	67,963	124,514
Indonesia	—	—	1,634	—	—	—	1,222	2,856
Iran	242	28	—	10	—	40	—	320
Iraq	172	—	—	—	—	—	—	172
Israel	195,875	7	—	—	—	235	191	196,308
Japan	2,336,813	393	—	31	1,334	30	—	2,338,601
Jordan	341	19	—	—	—	—	—	360
Korea, Republic of	1,021	—	—	814	—	6	58,766	60,607
Kuwait	839	—	—	39	20	2	—	900
Laos	—	—	31	—	—	—	1,684	1,715
Lebanon	51,515	23	—	11	—	13	—	51,562
Malaysia	220	—	—	—	—	—	43	263
Nansei and Nanpo Islands	2,352	—	—	—	—	89	—	2,441
Pakistan	9	—	—	—	—	—	—	9
Philippines	3,169	5	—	63	—	759	2,399	6,395
Saudi Arabia	1,210	—	—	20	—	38	—	1,268
Singapore	86	—	—	6	—	—	—	92
South Viet-Nam	31,504	—	—	—	—	81	5,149	36,734
Syrian Arab Republic	58	6	—	—	—	—	—	64
Taiwan	18,311	—	—	—	—	152	—	18,463
Thailand	70	—	—	—	—	12	—	82
Total	2,705,817	509	1,665	1,000	1,354	1,897	137,691	2,849,933
Oceania:								
Australia	1,754	—	—	—	3,908	1,990	37	7,689
New Zealand	92	18	—	—	—	134	404	648
British Western Pacific Islands ...	—	—	—	—	—	—	404	404
French Pacific Islands	—	—	—	—	—	16	—	16
Trust Territory of the Pacific Islands	—	1	—	—	—	11	—	12
Total	1,846	19	—	—	3,908	2,151	845	8,769
World Total	16,968,757	11,562	7,862	65,428	39,077	57,249	268,008	17,417,943
Equivalent, 1,000 bushels	668,023	455	310	2,576	1,538	2,254	10,551	685,707

1/ Adjusted to cover transhipments through Canadian ports which are included in data for countries of ultimate destination. 2/ Less than .5 metric tons.

COARSE GRAINS (grain equivalent): U.S. exports by country of destination, fiscal year 1965-66

Oats	Oatmeal and groats, nec.	Oatmeal to be cooked	Total	Barley	Malt	Total	Grain sorghums	Grand total all grains & products	Destination
Metric tons	Metric tons	Metric tons	Metric tons	Metric tons	Metric tons	Metric tons	Metric tons	Metric tons	
									:Africa:
—	—	—	—	—	—	—	—	17	Algeria
—	—	—	—	—	—	—	43	302	Angola
—	—	—	—	—	—	—	—	380	Burundi and Rwanda
—	—	—	—	—	—	—	7,595	95,038	Canary Islands
—	—	—	—	3,187	3,187	—	—	5,411	Congo (Kinshasa)
—	—	7	7	—	—	—	12,499	12,819	Ethiopia
—	—	—	—	—	—	—	1,043	1,043	French Somaliland
—	—	—	—	—	—	—	12	3,904	Ghana
—	—	—	—	—	—	—	99	199	Guinea
—	—	—	—	—	—	—	—	994	Ivory Coast
—	—	—	—	—	—	—	7,207	190,096	Kenya
—	—	—	—	—	6	6	—	1,141	Liberia
—	—	1	1	—	—	—	—	102	Libya
—	—	2/	2/	—	—	—	—	3,734	Malagasy Republic
—	—	—	—	—	—	—	—	16	Malawi
—	—	18	18	—	—	—	—	43,242	Morocco
—	—	—	—	—	—	—	—	584	Mozambique
—	—	—	—	—	—	—	—	1,755	Nigeria
—	—	—	—	—	—	—	—	1,308	Rhodesia
—	—	—	—	—	—	—	2,400	17,393	Senegal
—	—	—	—	—	—	—	—	2,317	Sierra Leone
—	—	—	—	—	—	—	4,992	6,354	Somali Republic
9	—	—	9	—	—	—	855	173,558	South Africa, Republic of
—	—	—	—	—	—	—	—	3	Spanish Africa, n.e.c.
—	—	—	—	—	—	—	1,866	23,370	Tanzania
—	—	—	—	—	—	—	—	1,927	Togo
—	—	—	—	7,827	—	7,827	—	25,913	Tunisia
—	—	—	—	—	—	—	—	195	Uganda
—	—	—	—	—	—	—	1,747	10,337	United Arab Republic
—	—	—	—	—	—	—	7,855	10,120	Western Africa, n.e.c.
—	—	—	—	—	—	—	—	325	Zambia
9	—	26	35	7,827	3,193	11,020	48,213	633,897	Total
									:Asia:
—	—	—	—	—	—	—	—	121	Aden
—	—	—	—	—	—	—	—	1	Afghanistan
—	—	—	—	—	—	—	—	372	Arabian Peninsula States
—	—	—	—	—	—	—	—	104	Bahrein
—	—	—	—	—	—	—	—	98	Ceylon
—	3	—	3	—	—	—	1,000	6,514	Hong Kong
—	—	—	—	—	4	4	1,037,551	1,162,069	India
—	—	1	1	9	—	9	—	2,856	Indonesia
—	—	—	—	—	—	—	—	330	Iran
—	—	—	—	—	—	—	172	344	Iraq
508	—	—	508	42,673	—	42,673	254,680	493,661	Israel
—	—	2/	2/	261,397	—	261,397	1,833,750	4,434,256	Japan
—	—	—	—	—	—	—	—	360	Jordan
—	—	1	1	8,000	—	8,000	—	68,608	Korea, Republic of
—	—	—	—	—	—	—	—	900	Kuwait
—	—	—	—	—	—	—	—	1,715	Laos
—	—	—	—	—	—	—	4,932	56,494	Lebanon
—	—	—	—	—	—	—	—	263	Malaysia
—	4	—	4	—	—	—	2,246	4,691	Nansei and Nanpo Islands
—	—	—	—	—	—	—	12	21	Pakistan
91	—	—	91	—	229	229	1,999	8,714	Philippines
—	—	—	—	—	—	—	—	1,272	Saudi Arabia
—	—	4	4	—	—	—	—	92	Singapore
—	—	—	—	—	—	1	1,406	38,140	South Viet-Nam
—	—	—	—	—	—	—	—	64	Syrian Arab Republic
—	—	—	—	—	2	2	—	18,465	Taiwan
—	—	—	—	—	—	—	—	82	Thailand
599	7	6	612	312,079	235	312,314	3,137,748	6,300,607	Total
									:Oceania:
—	—	—	—	16,764	—	16,764	5	24,458	Australia
—	—	—	—	—	—	—	—	648	New Zealand
—	—	—	—	—	113	113	—	404	British Western Pacific Islands
—	—	—	—	—	—	—	—	130	French Pacific Islands
—	—	1	1	—	—	—	—	12	Trust Territory of the Pacific Islands
—	—	1	1	16,764	113	16,877	5	25,652	Total
523,594	10,240	856	534,690	1,618,405	53,158	1,671,563	6,177,432	25,801,628	World Total
36,072	706	59	36,837	74,332	2,641	76,773	243,192	—	Equivalent, 1,000 bushels

Cornstarch shipments amounted to 48,000 tons compared with 57,000 tons for the same period a year earlier. This decrease was mostly due to smaller shipments to the two major markets, namely the United Kingdom and Canada.

Oatmeal - Exports of oatmeal totaled 25,000 tons compared with 11,000 tons last year. This large increase was attributed mostly to greater shipments to Colombia and South Vietnam.

Barley Malt - Malt exports totaled 52,000 tons compared with 53,000 tons a year earlier. Venezuela was by far the largest market and accounted for 58 percent of the total malt exported.

UNITED STATES DEPARTMENT OF AGRICULTURE

WASHINGTON 25, D. C.

———————

Official Business

GRAIN
U. S. DEPT. OF AGRICULTURE   FG 2-68
NATIONAL AGRICULTURAL LIBRARY   March 1968

WORLD BREADGRAIN CROP

APPROXIMATES 1966 RECORD

World breadgrain production in 1967 is close to the sharply increased
level of 1966 and 8 percent above the previous largest harvest of 1964,
according to the second estimate of Foreign Agricultural Service. Increased rye production about offset a decline of only 1 percent in wheat.

Combined estimates of world wheat and rye crops in 1967 total 309 million
metric tons compared with 310 million in 1966. Production is 17 percent
above the average production of 264 million tons in 1960-64.

The sharp gain in breadgrain production in the 1960's has been due to
considerable success in efforts to increase wheat output. Estimated
world wheat acreage in 1967, at 528 million acres, is 25 million more
than the average of 1960-64. Also, improved cultivation methods in
many countries have gradually increased average yields harvested per acre.

World _wheat_ production in 1967, estimated at 277 million metric tons
(10.2 bil. bu.), is only slightly under the September estimate of 278
million tons, and compares with 280 million tons (10.3 bil. bu.) in
1966. Record production prior to 1966 was 255 million tons (9.4 bil.
bu.) in 1964; average output during the 5 years ended 1964 was 232
million tons (8.5 bil. bu.).

The bumper wheat crops of 1967 were harvested in different world areas
than in 1966. The largest increases over 1966 occurred in Western Europe
and Asia, and South American prospects are for the largest crop in years.
North America just about held at the preceding year's increased level.
Oceania's harvest declined sharply and is below average.

WHEAT: Area, yield per acre, and production in specified countries, year of harvest, average 1960-64, annual 67 1/

Continent and Country	Acreage				Yield per acre				Production					
	Average 1960-64 1,000 acres	1965 1,000 acres	1966 1,000 acres	1967 2/ 1,000 acres	Average 1960-64 Bushels	1965 Bushels	1966 Bushels	1967 2/ Bushels	Average 1960-64 1,000 m.t.	1965 1,000 m.t.	1966 1,00 m.t.	1967 2/ 1,00 m.t.	1966 Million bushels 4/	1967 2/ Million 4/ bushels
North Amer:														
Ca	26,785	8,82	29,692	30,121	20.1	22.9	27.9	19.7	14,649	17,661	22,957	16,137	827.3	592.9
Mex	48,481	49,560	49,867	59,024	25.2	26.5	26.3	25.8	33,254	35,806	35,699	41,489	1,311.7	1,524.3
es	1,971	2,093	1,688	2,123	25.4	36.7	35.0	38.8	1,277	2,088	2,240	2,240	59.1	82.3
Total 5/	77,325	80,030	81,343	91,346	23.5	25.5	27.0	24.1	49,505	55,584	59,856	59,889	2,199.0	2,200.0
Sh Amer:														
A	11,651	11,89	12,883	14,580	22.6	20.1	18.2	19.7	7,164	6,200	6,380	7,800	234.4	286.6
B	1,395	87			6.5	9.6			227	230	50	90	12.9	12.9
B	2,090	1,98	1,813	1,850	21.3	22.2	23.8	22.8	1,213	1,87	1,174	1,150	43.1	42.3
Br	350	297	272	185	13.1	17.3	16.9	17.9	125	140	125	80	4.6	3.3
Pu	166	170	61	161	13.7	14.2	13.0	13.7	62	66	57	60	2.1	2.2
Uruguay	377	90	90	370	14.6	14.7	13.9	13.9	48	48	40	60	5.1	5.1
El 2/	1,107	1,302	1,200		14.4	15.4	15.2		547	547	420	211	5.1	7.7
El 2/	17,378	16,552	17,946	19,486	20.0	19.1	17.9	18.6	9,467	8,582	8,732	9,875	321.0	363.0
Europe:														
E	93	562	525	492	57.1	55.8	45.5	61.9	98	84	60	829	23.9	30.5
Be	10,459	11,71	9,865	9,721	41.3	48.5	42.1	54.4	11,746	14,760	11,297	14,383	415.1	528.5
Ay, West	3,430	3,89	3,81	3,85	50.7	45.8	48.5	61.2	4,731	4,18	4,533	5,819	166.6	213.8
Luxembourg	11,000	10,602	10,561	9,912	27.6	33.9	32.7	35.4	8,261	9,777	9,406	9,50	345.5	350.9
Netherlands	48	45	42	38	38	36.5	36.5	36.2	46	46	39	58	1.4	2.1
El EEC	326	292	366	381	65.8	64.8	60.0	48.0	583	691	597	729	22.2	27.2
	25,776	26,292	24,790	24,039	42.4	44.5	39.4	42.0	26,163	30,476	26,522	31,378	424.5	1,153.0
Austria	63	75	75	782	38.3	35.6	42.5	69	712	661	98	33.0	36.7	
Denmark	299	33	231	225	59.8	66.2	66	68.8	87	64	80	421	47	15.5
	98	60	96	623	25.9	27.9	26.3	29.9	422	61	89	67	13.5	18.6
Ireland	2,690	2,776	2,515	2,315	23.5	26.3	28.6	29.3	1,722	85	1,959	88	72.0	67.9
Norway	294	182	31	86	43.9	42.3	45.2	42.5	206	112	60	229	5.9	8.4
	21	10	4		38.0	43.3	38.0	44.5	22	4	10		0.2	0.4
	1,754	1,552	1,211	1,606	11.8	16.5	9.3	13.8	526	612	66	66	11.2	20.8
	10,251	10,380	10,380	10,543	11.0	14.5	18.8	44.8	4,128	4,716	4,813	5,04	176.8	198.6
El	83	64	472	67	46.1	55.8	44.8	65.2	88	1,038	96	1,05	21.2	40.2
	257	256	259	250	49.0	48.1	45.4	48.5	33	35	320	30	11.8	12.1
Wn Europe 5/	3,064	2,535	2,238	2,306	58.6	60.5	57.1	62.3	3,293	4,171	3,475	3,912	127.7	143.7
	45,375	46,427	43,527	43,511	31.6	25.8	39.6	39.4	39,016	43,284	39,804	46,701	1,631.0	1,716.7
Albania	283				12.8				99					
Bulgaria	3,057	2,829	2,817	2,619	25.2	37.9	41.4	44.9	2,100	2,921	3,173	3, 80	116.6	117.6
Czechoslovakia	1,739	2,041	2,195	2,278	35.5	35.9	37.9	40.3	1,682	1,992	2,266	2, 80	83.3	91.9
Germany, East	1,027	1,213	1,196	1,260	46.1	54.6	46.7	49.6	1,288	1,892	2,521	2,722	55.9	62.5
Hungary	2,942	2,674	2,508	2,497	26.2	32.2	38.2	38.2	2,97	2,36	2,191	3,916	80.5	100.0
	3,626	4,103	4,198	4,324	28.2	30.6	31.9	34.3	2,97	3,422	3,646	3,916	134.0	143.9
	7,256	7,371	4,198	4,86	19.5	29.6	24.9	29.9	3,823	5,97	5,065	5,800	186.1	213.1
Yugoslavia	5,135	4,151	4,522	1,645	25.9	30.6	37.4	38.1	3,618	3,460	4,600	4,820	169.0	177.1
Ern Europe 5/	24,717	24,682	25,233	25,199	25.6	32.7	32.9	36.1	17,239	21,980	22,562	24,758	829.0	190.0
Total Europe 5/	70,092	71,109	68,760	68,710	29.5	34.8	33.3	38.2	56,255	61,264	62,366	71,459	2,232.0	2,626.0
U.S.S.R.	160,000	173,500	173,000	162,000	11.5	9.9	17.0	14.7	50,000	46,500	80,000	63,000	2,940.0	2,315.0
Total (Europe and Asia) 6/														

- 2 -

1/ Years shown refer to ms of harvest in the Northern Hemisphere. Harvests of Northern Hemisphere countries ms combined th those of the Southern Hemisphere
follow; thus, the mp harvested in the Northern Hemisphere in 1967 is combined with preliminary ms for me Southern Hemisph re harvests, which begin late in 1967 and
end ny in 8. 2/ Harvested ms as far as possible. 3/ Preliminary. 4/ me converted to bushels at 36.7433. 5/ Estim.ms ed ms include allowances for
producing countries not shown. 6/ Production.

Foreign Agricultural Service. Prepared or md on the ms of md on the ms of md information.
Attaches and Fore gn ms Officers. ms of office research, md information.

RYE: Acreage, yield per acre, and production in specified countries, year of harvest, average 1960-64, annual 1965-67 1/

Continent and Country	Acreage 2/				Yield per acre				Production					
	Average 1960-64	1965	1966	1967 3/	Average 1960-64	1965	1966	1967 3/	Average 1960-64	1965	1966	1967 3/	1966	1967 3/
	1,000 acres	1,000 acres	1,000 acres	1,000 acres	Bushels	Bushels	Bushels	Bushels	1,000 m.t.	1,000 m.t.	1,000 m.t.	1,000 m.t.	Million 4/ bushels	Million 4/ bushels
North America:														
Canada	616	746	726	758	17.5	22.4	23.7	17.5	274	424	437	337	17.2	13.3
United States	1,699	1,469	1,275	1,072	19.2	22.6	21.8	22.5	827	844	706	612	27.8	24.1
Total	2,315	2,215	2,001	1,830	18.7	22.5	22.5	20.4	1,101	1,268	1,143	949	45.0	37.4
South America:														
Argentina	1,553	818	1,039	---	12.0	11.8	10.2	---	474	245	270	420	10.6	16.5
Europe:														
EEC:														
Belgium	112	85	74	68	48.4	45.2	40.2	52.8	138	98	76	91	3.0	3.6
France	628	516	487	456	23.7	27.0	28.8	31.0	373	387	356	362	14.0	14.2
Germany, West	2,905	2,787	2,522	2,408	43.7	39.9	47.0	50.7	3,225	2,825	2,696	3,162	106.1	124.5
Italy	139	118	115	118	25.2	27.8	28.5	27.2	89	83	83	82	3.3	3.2
Luxembourg	8	12	6	8	34.1	34.4	44.7	40.9	7	10	7	8	0.3	0.3
Netherlands	291	242	183	181	47.9	40.7	41.0	52.0	354	290	190	239	7.5	9.4
Total EEC	4,075	3,790	3,387	3,242	40.4	37.9	39.6	47.9	4,186	3,653	3,408	3,944	134.2	155.2
Austria	451	387	356	342	35.0	32.1	40.2	41.4	401	316	363	360	14.3	14.2
Denmark	356	216	114	89	46.3	48.3	47.0	52.2	418	265	136	118	5.4	4.6
Finland	230	273	230	238	24.0	27.4	20.3	27.0	140	190	119	163	4.7	6.4
Greece	59	40	32	27	15.9	18.7	18.7	20.4	24	19	15	14	.6	.6
Norway	3	2	2	2	39.0	32.0	32.5	40.5	3	2	1	2	..	..
Portugal	745	782	645	647	8.6	10.5	10.2	14.3	163	209	168	234	6.6	9.2
Spain	1,157	971	961	954	13.4	14.1	14.6	12.8	393	349	357	309	14.0	12.2
Sweden	160	149	97	149	37.8	45.3	34.3	51.0	154	171	85	193	3.3	7.6
Switzerland	37	44	40	40	54.8	52.3	55.1	58.1	51	98	56	59	2.2	2.2
United Kingdom	19	18	10	11	42.1	40.7	44.1	43.6	20	25	11	11	..	..
Total Western Europe 5/	7,294	6,674	5,874	5,743	32.1	31.0	31.6	37.1	5,955	5,255	4,721	5,410	186.0	213.0
Bulgaria	160	114	104	100	15.6	18.0	21.2	34.4	64	82	56	50	2.2	2.0
Czechoslovakia	1,071	1,013	976	793	33.5	31.0	33.9	33.8	911	822	794	691	31.3	27.2
Germany, East	2,088	2,031	1,905	1,980	31.3	37.0	33.9	33.8	1,784	1,910	1,642	1,700	64.6	66.9
Hungary	621	607	543	519	17.3	18.6	17.5	17.1	273	288	242	225	9.5	8.9
Poland	11,615	11,104	10,813	10,100	25.1	29.4	28.3	29.5	7,405	8,289	7,700	7,500	306.2	295.3
Romania	216	253	225	210	18.7	19.5	19.2	18.7	91	125	100	100	3.9	3.9
Yugoslavia	437	361	348	341	19.8	17.0	19.9	19.8	185	156	176	177	6.9	7.0
Total Eastern Europe 5/	16,233	15,505	14,936	13,065	26.0	29.6	28.4	29.4	10,719	11,648	10,709	10,462	421.5	411.7
Total Europe 5/	23,527	22,179	20,810	19,708	27.9	30.0	29.3	31.7	16,674	16,903	15,514	15,852	611.0	624.0
U.S.S.R. (Europe and Asia) 6/	40,340	39,530	33,600	37,100	13.0	14.5	14.1	15.2	13,300	14,500	12,000	14,300	472.0	563.0
Asia:														
Turkey 1/	1,560	1,800	1,810	1,815	17.0	15.3	17.0	17.9	672	700	780	825	30.7	32.5
World Total 4/	69,650	66,900	59,600	62,100	18.3	19.8	19.7	20.6	32,300	33,700	29,800	32,400	1,173.0	1,277.0

1/ Years shown refer to years of harvest in the Northern Hemisphere. Harvests of the Northern Hemisphere in 1967 is combined with preliminary forecasts for the Southern Hemisphere harvests, which begin late in 1967 and end early in 1968. 2/ Harvested acreage as far as possible. 3/ Preliminary. 4/ Production estimated. 5/ Metric tons converted to bushels at 39.368. 6/ Estimated totals include allowances for producing countries not shown.

Foreign Agricultural Service. Prepared or estimated on the basis of official statistics of foreign governments, other foreign source materials, reports of U.S. Agricultural Attaches and Foreign Service Officers, results of office research, and related information.

The USSR produced a near-record crop, although substantially below the 1966 record. Combined acreage of the winter and spring wheat crops was 6. percent below that of 1966. Winter wheat was a very good crop. However, dryness at the outset of the growing season reduced spring wheat yields.

Wheat yields per acre in Western Europe were at a previously unheard of high level. Climate was unusually favorable during 1967. Despite another year of reduced winter acreage by wet, freezing weather in late 1966, record wheat production was 17 percent above the preceding year. It topped by 3 percent the previous record of 1965, when wheat acreage was nearly 3 million acres higher.

Record production of the EEC countries reached 31.38 million metric tons compared with 26.52 million in 1966, and the average of 26.16 million in 1960-64. Average yields per acre for the six countries was 13 percent higher than the previous record of 1965. Although acreage of France, Italy, Belgium and Luxembourg was well below average, the unusually high yields brought in near-record crops. West Germany and the Netherlands, with above average acreage, produced by far the largest crops on record. Spain, the United Kingdom, Greece, Sweden and other European countries also produced bumper crops.

Wheat acreage in countries of Eastern Europe was nearly at the high level of 1966. High yields harvested resulted in larger crops than in 1966 and far above the average.

Prospective total production of the five main exporting countries--Argentina, Australia, Canada, France, and the United States--is close to the 1966 record. Production increases in the United States, France, and Argentina offset sharp declines in the harvests of Canada and Australia.

Despite unfavorable weather in some areas of the United States that reduced the average yields per acre, a substantial rise in wheat acreage resulted in a large increase in that country's production. This, together with a bumper crop in Mexico, offset the sharp decline in the production of Canada, and maintained North America's production at about the 1966 record level. Although Canada planted a record acreage, drought hit the wheat fields during the crucial growing stage. Only good subsoil moisture made possible the reasonable good yields per acre harvested.

Wet, freezing weather in the second successive year kept the French wheat acreage at the lowest level in four years. Yet, yields far superior to any previously produced resulted in a near-record crop.

Argentina planted the largest wheat acreage in 21 years. However, weather has been unfavorable in some areas. The crop is expected to be well above average, but not nearly as large as the record crop of 11,260,000 tons of 1964.

The worst drought in Australia in years caused a sharp drop in wheat output. Although farmers planted a record acreage, production is forecast at only about 60 percent of the preceding year's record crop, and 9 percent below the average.

Countries of the Near East produced exceptionally good crops in 1967. Acreage increased substantially in Iran, Turkey, Jordan, and Israel, and yields per acre higher than normal. Crops of India and Pakistan were markedly better than in 1966, but not up to the 1965 record harvests. Afghanistan had a very good crop.

Weather was more favorable for production of North African countries and crops were far larger than the poor harvests of 1966. South Africa has a near-record crop, almost as large as the 1964 record.

World rye production in 1967, at 32.4 million metric tons, is 9 percent larger than in 1966, and only slightly above the average. Acreage declined in the 1960's, with acreage in 1967 about 11 percent below the average. But record yields per acre in Western Europe and a good crop in the USSR resulted in a world crop slightly above the 1960-64 average.

Total acreage of Eastern Europe--producing nearly a third of the world rye--decline 7 percent from 1966 and was 14 percent below the average in 1960-64. Though yields per acre were at a high level, East European production was 3 percent below the 1966 crop.

POSTAGE AND FEES PAID
U. S. DEPARTMENT OF AGRICULTURE

GRAIN
FG 3-68
April 1968

WORLD BREADGRAIN PRODUCTION

NEAR TOP LEVEL IN 1967

The third estimate of world breadgrain production in 1967, at 310.7 million metric tons (11.5 bil. bu.) approximates the first estimate of 310.8 million tons (11.51 bil. bu.) released by the Foreign Agricultural Service last September. Both wheat and rye crops are confirmed at the September estimates.

The revised estimate of 315.3 million tons (11.66 bil. bu.) for 1966 breadgrain production reflects an upward adjustment of 5 million tons in the wheat crop of the USSR. This estimate is based on currently available information and has not been adjusted to reflect estimated above average losses.

World acreage in breadgrains increased 11 million to a record 591 million acres, 19 million more than the average of 1960-64. Wheat acreage, at 529 million acres, was 8 million larger than in 1966, and 26 million more than during the 5 years ended 1964. Nearly 63 million acres in rye showed an increase of 3 million over the preceding year, but were 7 million below the average.

Major Continents Harvested Record Wheat Crop

World wheat production in 1967 in all countries except the USSR and Mainland China totaled 190 million metric tons. This was 10 million tons above the previous record of 180 million in 1966 and 30 million larger than the average output during the 5 years ended 1964. The upward surge was due to increased acreage in some areas, unusually favorable weather in other lands, and generally improved production methods all over the world.

WHEAT: Acreage, yield per acre, and production in specified countries, year of harvest, average 1960-64, annual 1966 and 1967 1/

Continent and country	Acreage			Yield per acre			Production				
	Average 1960-64	1966	1967 2/	Average 1960-64	1966	1967 2/	Average 1960-64	1966	1967 2/	1966	1967 2/
	1,000 acres	1,000 acres	1,000 acres	Bushels	Bushels	Bushels	1,000 m.t.	1,000 m.t.	1,000 m.t.	Million 4/ bushels	Million 4/ bushels
North America:											
Canada	26,785	29,692	30,121	20.1	27.9	19.7	14,643	22,517	16,137	827.3	592.9
United States	48,481	49,867	59,004	25.2	26.3	25.8	33,254	35,699	41,487	1,311.7	1,524.3
Mexico	1,971	1,569	2,123	29.4	37.7	38.8	1,577	1,609	2,240	59.1	82.3
Guatemala	83	91	93	10.6	12.1	9.5	24	30	24	1.1	0.9
Total 2/	77,325	81,224	91,346	23.5	27.1	24.1	49,505	59,856	59,889	2,199.0	2,200.0
South America:											
Argentina	11,651	12,883	14,581	22.6	17.8	17.6	7,164	6,247	7,000	129.5	257.2
Brazil	1,015	865	890	8.9	14.9	15.7	247	350	380	12.9	14.0
Chile	2,090	1,775	1,770	21.3	24.9	24.8	1,213	1,204	1,196	44.2	44.0
Colombia	350	272	168	13.0	16.9	17.5	124	125	80	4.6	2.9
Ecuador	166	161	161	13.7	13.0	13.7	62	57	60	2.1	2.2
Peru	377	370	370	14.6	13.9	13.9	150	140	140	5.1	5.1
Uruguay	1,177	1,200	300	14.6	12.8	13.9	424	420	140	15.6	5.1
Total 2/	16,998	17,772	18,880	20.5	17.8	17.7	9,466	8,629	9,120	317.0	335.0
Europe:											
EEC:											
Belgium	513	525	492	57.1	45.5	61.9	798	650	830	23.9	30.5
France	10,459	9,865	9,721	41.3	42.1	54.4	11,746	11,297	14,383	415.1	528.5
Germany, West	3,430	3,431	3,495	50.7	48.5	61.2	4,731	4,533	5,819	166.6	213.8
Italy	11,008	10,562	9,913	27.6	36.5	35.5	8,261	9,406	9,564	345.4	351.4
Luxembourg	42	42	38	33.9	36.0	36.2	22	58	58	2.1	2.1
Netherlands	326	366	381	65.8	60.0	71.2	583	577	739	22.0	27.1
Total EEC	25,776	24,790	24,040	37.3	39.3	48.0	26,163	26,522	31,393	974.5	1,153.4
Austria	683	775	782	38.3	42.5	49.2	712	897	1,045	33.0	38.4
Denmark	299	231	225	59.8	63.6	68.8	487	400	421	14.7	15.5
Finland	598	516	623	25.9	26.3	29.9	422	369	507	13.6	18.6
Greece	2,690	2,515	2,315	23.5	28.6	29.3	1,722	1,959	1,848	72.0	67.9
Ireland	294	131	189	43.9	47.0	48.4	351	168	249	6.2	9.1
Norway	21	4	8	38.0	38.0	48.6	22	4	11	.2	.4
Portugal	1,754	1,211	1,606	11.0	9.3	13.0	526	306	566	11.2	20.8
Spain	10,251	10,380	10,549	17.3	17.3	19.5	4,120	4,876	5,598	179.2	205.7
Sweden	683	472	633	46.1	44.8	65.5	858	576	1,128	21.2	41.4
Switzerland	257	259	255	49.0	47.9	62.2	343	338	432	12.4	15.9
United Kingdom	2,064	2,238	2,305	58.6	57.1	62.4	3,293	3,475	3,512	127.7	143.7
Total Western Europe 5/	45,375	43,527	43,535	31.6	33.7	39.8	39,022	39,803	47,113	1,466.0	1,731.0
Albania	283	—	—	12.8			99				
Bulgaria	3,057	2,822	2,619	25.2	41.6	44.9	2,100	3,193	3,200	117.3	117.6
Czechoslovakia	1,739	2,204	2,296	35.5	37.5	40.0	1,682	2,247	2,500	82.6	91.9
Germany, East	1,027	1,196	1,260	46.1	46.7	49.6	1,288	1,521	1,700	55.9	62.5
Hungary	2,594	2,508	2,609	26.2	32.1	38.3	1,849	2,192	2,716	80.5	99.8
Poland	3,619	4,198	4,324	28.2	31.9	33.3	2,781	3,646	3,916	134.0	143.9
Romania	7,256	7,497	7,166	19.5	24.9	29.7	3,823	5,065	3,800	186.1	213.1
Yugoslavia	5,135	4,522	4,645	25.9	32.8	38.1	3,618	4,600	4,820	169.0	177.1
Total Eastern Europe 5/	24,710	25,247	25,219	25.6	32.8	36.1	17,240	22,564	24,752	829.0	910.0
Total Europe 5/	70,085	68,774	68,754	29.5	33.4	38.4	56,262	62,457	71,865	2,295.0	2,641.0
U.S.S.R. (Europe and Asia) 6/	160,000	173,000	162,600	11.5	18.1	14.7	50,000	85,000	65,000	3,123.0	2,388.0

Africa:	:		:		:		:		:		:		:		:		:		:	
Algeria	:	4,733	:	3,656	:	—	:	10.0	:	7.3	:	—	:	1,290	:	722	:	1,350	:	26.5	:	49.6
Ethiopia	:	914	:	—	:	—	:	10.5	:	—	:	—	:	260	:	—	:	—	:	—	:	—
Morocco	:	3,905	:	4,043	:	4,389	:	9.7	:	7.4	:	9.1	:	1,036	:	812	:	1,090	:	29.8	:	40.0
Sudan	:	47	:	141	:	—	:	23.0	:	20.3	:	—	:	30	:	78	:	93	:	2.9	:	3.4
Tunisia	:	2,661	:	2,088	:	2,014	:	6.0	:	6.1	:	6.0	:	432	:	349	:	330	:	12.8	:	12.1
United Arab Republic	:	1,440	:	1,340	:	1,450	:	38.4	:	40.2	:	38.0	:	1,504	:	1,465	:	1,500	:	53.8	:	55.1
Kenya	:	267	:	340	:	377	:	16.2	:	19.5	:	20.0	:	117	:	180	:	205	:	6.6	:	7.5
South Africa, Republic of	:	2,851	:	2,463	:	3,050	:	11.1	:	8.5	:	12.7	:	861	:	567	:	1,052	:	20.8	:	38.7
Total 5/	:	17,651	:	16,003	:	18,397	:	11.9	:	10.7	:	12.3	:	5,696	:	4,648	:	6,141	:	171.0	:	226.0
Asia:	:		:		:		:		:		:		:		:		:		:	
Cyprus	:	178	:	150	:	146	:	10.8	:	13.1	:	23.0	:	52	:	53	:	91	:	2.0	:	3.4
Iran	:	4,925	:	5,300	:	—	:	20.4	:	22.1	:	—	:	2,740	:	3,190	:	3,800	:	117.2	:	139.6
Iraq	:	3,060	:	—	:	—	:	8.7	:	—	:	—	:	726	:	630	:	700	:	23.1	:	25.7
Israel	:	128	:	189	:	222	:	19.5	:	19.6	:	36.4	:	68	:	101	:	220	:	3.7	:	8.1
Jordan	:	604	:	529	:	674	:	8.1	:	7.0	:	13.5	:	133	:	101	:	248	:	3.7	:	9.1
Lebanon	:	142	:	146	:	150	:	9.8	:	15.1	:	17.1	:	38	:	60	:	70	:	2.2	:	2.6
Turkey	:	16,400	:	17,700	:	17,800	:	15.6	:	17.0	:	18.6	:	6,980	:	8,200	:	9,000	:	301.3	:	330.7
Syria	:	2,750	:	2,800	:	—	:	9.7	:	5.2	:	—	:	728	:	400	:	600	:	14.7	:	22.0
China, Mainland	:	62,500	:	60,500	:	60,500	:	12.7	:	12.6	:	14.0	:	21,600	:	20,800	:	23,000	:	764.0	:	845.0
Afghanistan	:	5,700	:	5,800	:	—	:	14.3	:	12.8	:	—	:	2,200	:	2,023	:	2,400	:	74.3	:	88.2
India	:	33,123	:	31,272	:	32,457	:	12.0	:	12.2	:	13.1	:	10,809	:	10,424	:	11,528	:	383.0	:	423.6
Japan	:	1,475	:	1,014	:	909	:	34.4	:	37.1	:	40.0	:	1,381	:	1,024	:	991	:	37.6	:	36.4
Korea, South	:	328	:	378	:	375	:	30.1	:	30.7	:	30.4	:	269	:	315	:	310	:	11.6	:	11.4
Nepal	:	330	:	290	:	305	:	15.0	:	22.1	:	22.5	:	135	:	175	:	187	:	6.4	:	6.9
Pakistan	:	12,301	:	12,874	:	13,385	:	12.1	:	11.3	:	12.1	:	4,065	:	3,951	:	4,393	:	145.2	:	161.4
Total 5/	:	144,822	:	143,196	:	145,462	:	13.3	:	13.3	:	14.6	:	52,295	:	51,904	:	57,989	:	1,907.0	:	2,131.0
Oceania:	:		:		:		:		:		:		:		:		:		:	
Australia	:	15,805	:	20,823	:	22,800	:	19.3	:	22.4	:	12.3	:	8,298	:	12,699	:	7,620	:	466.6	:	280.0
New Zealand	:	197	:	234	:	288	:	46.3	:	50.0	:	50.0	:	248	:	318	:	392	:	11.7	:	14.4
Total	:	16,002	:	21,057	:	23,088	:	19.6	:	22.7	:	12.8	:	8,546	:	13,017	:	8,012	:	478.0	:	294.0
	:		:		:		:		:		:		:		:		:		:	
World Total 5/	:	502,900	:	521,000	:	528,500	:	16.9	:	20.1	:	19.3	:	231,800	:	285,500	:	278,000	:	10,490.0	:	10,200.0

1/ Years shown refer to years of harvest in the Northern Hemisphere. Harvests of Northern Hemisphere countries are combined with those of the Southern Hemisphere which immediately follow; thus, the crop harvested in the Northern Hemisphere in 1967 is combined with preliminary forecast for the Southern Hemisphere harvests, which begin late in 1967 and end early in 1968. 2/ Harvested acreage as far as possible. 3/ Preliminary. 4/ Metric tons converted to bushels at 36.7433. 5/ Estimated totals include allowances for producing countries not shown. 6/ Production estimated. 7/ It is estimated post harvest losses were likely 5 million tons above normal and therefore the quantity available for utilization was reduced accordingly.

Foreign Agricultural Service. Prepared or estimated on the basis of official statistics of foreign governments, other foreign source materials, reports of U.S. Agricultural Attaches and Foreign Service Officers, results of office research, and related information.

RYE: Acreage, yield per acre, and production in specified countries, year of harvest, average 1960-64, annual 1966 and 1967 1/

Continent and country	Acreage Average 1960-64 (1,000 acres)	Acreage 1966 (1,000 acres)	Acreage 1967 2/ (1,000 acres)	Yield Average 1960-64 (Bushels)	Yield 1966 (Bushels)	Yield 1967 2/ (Bushels)	Production Average 1960-64 (1,000 m.t.)	Production 1966 (1,000 m.t.)	Production 1967 2/ (1,000 m.t.)	1966 (Million bu 4/)	1967 2/ (Million bu 4/)
North America:											
Canada	616	726	758	17.5	23.7	17.5	274	437	337	17.2	13.3
United States	1,699	1,275	1,072	19.2	21.8	22.5	827	706	612	27.8	24.1
Total	2,315	2,001	1,830	18.7	22.5	20.4	1,101	1,143	949	45.0	37.4
South America:											
Argentina	1,553	1,039	---	12.0	10.2	---	474	270	420	10.6	16.5
Europe:											
EEC:											
Belgium	112	74	68	48.4	40.2	52.2	138	76	90	3.0	3.6
France	620	487	459	23.7	28.8	31.0	373	356	362	14.0	14.2
Germany, West	2,905	2,522	2,408	43.7	42.1	51.7	3,225	2,696	3,162	106.1	124.5
Italy	139	115	113	25.2	28.5	28.4	89	83	82	3.3	3.2
Luxembourg	8	6	8	34.1	24.7	40.9	7	7	8	.3	.3
Netherlands	291	183	181	47.9	41.0	52.0	354	190	239	7.5	9.4
Total EEC	4,075	3,387	3,237	40.4	39.6	47.9	4,186	3,408	3,943	134.2	155.2
Austria	451	356	342	35.0	40.2	41.4	401	363	377	14.3	14.8
Denmark	356	114	91	46.3	47.0	51.0	418	136	118	5.4	4.6
Finland	230	230	238	24.0	20.3	26.9	140	119	163	4.7	6.4
Greece	59	32	27	15.9	18.7	20.4	24	15	14	.6	.6
Norway	3	1	2	39.0	32.5	45.5	3	2	2	--	.1
Portugal	745	645	647	8.6	10.2	12.4	163	168	204	6.6	8.0
Spain	1,157	961	954	13.4	14.6	12.7	393	357	309	14.0	12.2
Sweden	160	97	153	37.8	34.3	54.4	154	85	196	3.3	2.7
Switzerland	37	33	37	54.8	55.1	72.4	51	46	68	1.8	2.7
United Kingdom	19	10	11	42.1	44.1	43.6	20	11	12	.4	.5
Total Western Europe 5/	7,294	5,868	5,741	32.1	39.6	37.1	5,955	4,711	5,408	185.5	212.9
Bulgaria	160	104	100	15.6	21.2	19.7	64	56	50	2.2	2.0
Czechoslovakia	1,071	976	793	33.5	31.9	34.4	911	790	690	31.1	27.2
Germany, East	2,088	1,905	1,980	33.6	33.9	33.8	1,784	1,642	1,700	64.6	66.9
Hungary	621	543	519	17.3	17.5	17.1	273	242	225	9.5	8.9
Poland	11,608	10,813	10,625	25.1	28.3	28.5	7,401	7,777	7,700	306.2	303.1
Romania	216	225	210	16.5	19.2	24.3	91	100	130	3.9	5.1
Yugoslavia 5/	437	348	341	16.6	19.9	19.8	185	176	171	6.9	6.7
Total Eastern Europe 5/	16,226	14,936	14,590	26.0	28.4	28.8	10,715	10,789	10,672	424.7	420.1
Total Europe 5/	23,520	20,804	20,331	27.9	29.3	31.1	16,670	15,500	16,080	610.2	633.0
U.S.S.R. (Europe and Asia) 6/	40,340	33,600	37,100	13.0	14.1	15.2	13,330	12,000	14,300	472.0	563.0
Asia:											
Turkey	1,560	1,810	1,816	17.0	17.0	17.9	672	780	825	30.7	32.5
World Total 5/	69,650	59,600	62,700	18.3	19.7	20.5	32,350	29,800	32,700	1,173.0	1,287.0

1/ Years shown refer to years of harvest in the Northern Hemisphere. Harvests of Northern Hemisphere countries are combined with those of the Southern Hemisphere which immediately follow; thus, the crop in the Northern Hemisphere in 1967 is combined with preliminary forecast for the Southern Hemisphere harvests, which begin late in 1967 and early in 1968. 2/ Harvested as far as possible. 3/ Preliminary. 4/ Metric tons converted to bushels at 39.368. 5/ Estimated totals include allowances for producing countries not shown. 6/ Production estimated.

Foreign Agricultural Service. Prepared or estimated on the basis of official statistics of foreign governments, other foreign source materials, reports of U.S. Agricultural Attaches and Foreign Service Officers, results of office research, and related information.

World 1967 wheat acreage, excluding the USSR and Mainland China, increased 18 million acres from the year before to 305 million acres. The largest expansion took place in the United States, but nearly all the areas planted more acreage to wheat.

Major increases in production occurred in Western Europe, Asia, and Eastern Europe. South America planted more wheat, and production increased 6 percent. Despite a 12-percent increase in acreage of North America, adverse weather in Canada and, to a lesser degree, the United States prevented production from any more than barely surpassing the preceding year's record level.

Western Europe's record crop of 47.1 million tons was 18 percent larger than in 1966 on approximately the same size land area. Unusually favorable weather over the Continent and use of high-standard production methods resulted in the production of an average 6.1 bushels more per acre than in 1966.

Crops of the EEC countries totaled 31.39 million metric tons, compared with 26.52 million in 1966 and the average of 26.16 million tons in 1960-64. Record or near-record crops were raised in these countries despite an acreage slightly below the low 1966 level. Yields per acre on the average were nearly 9 bushels higher than in the year before.

Wheat output of the USSR--producer of nearly a fourth of the world's wheat--was above average but substantially less than the high-yielding crop of 1966. Conditions were again favorable for winter wheat, but dry weather adversely affected the spring crop.

Production in Eastern Europe, at 24.8 million tons, was 2.2 million larger than in 1966 and nearly 8 million more than the average during 1960-64. Acreage was about the same as in 1966, but average yields per acre were 3.3 bushels higher than in the year before.

Asian countries increased wheat acreage more than 2 million acres, and record yields per acre were harvested. Therefore, at 58 million tons, production was about 6 million more than in 1966. India, Pakistan, Afghanistan, Turkey, and Iran--the leading producers--harvested large crops.

Estimated wheat production of the five main exporting countries totaled 86.6 million tons, compared with 88.5 million in 1966 and the average of 75 million in 1960-64. Main increases were in the United States and France.

The United States increased acreage 18 percent, but lower yields harvested per acre resulted in a crop only 16 percent (5.8 million tons) more than in 1966. Severe cold, wet weather again limited French winter wheat acreage at about the reduced 1966 level. However, unusually favorable weather during growing and harvesting made possible a high-yielding crop more than 3 million tons larger than in 1966.

Argentina also sharply increased. But adverse weather resulted in reduced yields per acre for the second successive year. Currently estimated production is only 0.7 million tons more than in 1966. Drought severely reduced the crops of Canada and Australia although these countries increased acreage. Canada's production, with yields per acre a little below average, was 6.4 million tons below the excellent crop of 1966. Since Australia's yields per acre were the lowest in 10 years, production was 5 million tons below the record 1966 level and 8 percent below the average.

World rye production, estimated at 32.68 million metric tons, is up 10 percent from the preceding year and 1 percent from the 1960-64 average. The crop is nearly 250,000 tons above the previous estimate (January), largely because of an upward revision in the acreage of Poland and higher yields in Romania.

World rye acreage--62.7 million acres--was 5 percent above the preceding year but 10 percent below the average. The decline in acreage of recent years continued generally except in the USSR, the principal producer.

The increase in production in 1967 above 1966 and also above the 1960-64 average was due mainly to favorable weather in Europe and the USSR and to improved production methods in principal growing areas. Yields per acre were well above the average in the USSR, and Eastern and Western Europe, where nine-tenths of the world's rye is produced.

UNITED STATES DEPARTMENT OF AGRICULTURE

WASHINGTON 25, D. C.

Official Business

7633

GRAIN STOCKS IN EXPORTING

COUNTRIES GAIN 8 PERCENT

Grain stocks in the four principal exporting countries--the United States, Canada, Argentina, and Australia--on January 1, 1968, totaled 218 million metric tons. This was an 8 percent increase over the same date a year earlier, but only 2 percent above 1966, as estimated by the Foreign Agricultural Service. The stocks included are wheat, rye, barley, oats, and corn.

Wheat stocks in the four countries totaled 77.0 million tons, 6 percent over last year and 2 percent higher than 2 years ago. Corn stocks, at 109.8 million tons, were respectively 14 percent and 5 percent above 1967 and 1966. Oats supplies, at 15.6 million tons, were 9 percent below 1967, and barley, at 14.4 million tons, were down 2 percent. Rye stocks were unchanged at 1.5 million tons.

United States grain stocks totaled 156.6 million tons, 13 percent higher than a year earlier, but barely below the levels of 1966 and 1965. This year's increase was principally due to record 1967 crops of wheat and corn.

U.S. wheat stocks, at 32.9 million tons on January 1, 1968, were 15 percent above those held in 1967 although 10 percent below those of two years ago. U.S. corn supplies at 107.1 million tons were also up 15 percent over 1967 and 4 percent above 1966. Barley stocks, at 6.6 million tons, were up 3 percent while oats, at 9.4 million tons, and rye, at 705,000 tons, were each down 2 percent. The United States also held 18.6 million tons of grain sorghum on January 1, down 11 percent, because of heavy exports, despite a 7-percent larger 1967 crop.

GRAINS: Estimated Stocks in Principal Exporting Countries, January 1, 1950-68 1/

	1,000 m. t.	1,000 m. t.	1,000 m. t.	1,000 m. t.	1,000 m. t.	1,000 m. t.
United States:						
Average 1950-54	28,304	406	4,267	12,425	65,583	110,985
Average 1955-59	42,140	605	7,146	13,812	85,308	149,011
1960	51,029	508	7,860	11,118	110,337	180,852
1961	56,282	660	7,794	12,367	119,050	196,153
1962	53,968	483	7,315	11,249	114,173	187,188
1963	49,451	610	7,533	11,177	107,112	175,883
1964	43,926	381	7,250	11,220	111,354	174,131
1965	39,446	540	6,747	10,310	100,479	157,522
1966	36,360	732	6,549	11,067	102,650	157,358
1967	28,552	721	6,409	9,607	93,406	138,695
1968 2/	32,881	705	6,589	9,397	107,060	156,632
Canada:						
Average 1950-54	15,322	508	4,224	5,413	3/	25,467
Average 1955-59	23,759	549	5,613	5,774	3/	35,695
1960	23,133	305	5,704	5,090	3/	34,232
1961	25,446	356	5,400	5,398	3/	36,600
1962	18,234	203	3,484	4,318	3/	26,239
1963	20,820	229	3,767	6,354	3/	31,170
1964	24,603	305	5,334	6,710	3/	36,952
1965	22,260	376	4,480	5,726	1,003	33,845
1966	22,725	495	5,125	5,689	1,186	35,220
1967	25,529	526	6,520	5,117	1,219	38,911
1968 2/	27,313	408	6,271	4,475	1,448	39,915
Argentina:						
Average 1950-54	5,906	813	784	987	890	9,380
Average 1955-59	7,838	853	1,206	958	1,016	11,871
1960	7,076	965	1,160	1,016	1,397	11,614
1961	5,307	560	870	943	635	8,315
1962	5,715	533	827	870	1,143	9,088
1963	4,900	203	435	508	890	6,936
1964	9,335	533	1,197	1,030	890	12,985
1965	11,630	655	805	840	950	14,880
1966	8,807	256	400	486	1,160	11,109
1967	5,960	255	410	515	1,595	8,735
1968 2/	7,715	395	680	530	1,340	10,660
Australia:						
Average 1950-54	5,688	3/	653	668	3/	7,009
Average 1955-59	5,900	3/	949	964	3/	7,813
1960	6,668	3/	870	1,452	3/	8,990
1961	8,573	3/	1,415	1,626	3/	11,614
1962	6,940	3/	893	1,350	3/	9,183
1963	8,410	3/	1,002	1,524	3/	10,936
1964	8,790	3/	1,100	1,600	3/	11,490
1965	10,342	3/	1,168	1,850	3/	13,360
1966	7,275	3/	925	1,140	3/	9,340
1967	12,770	3/	1,474	1,905	3/	16,149
1968 2/	9,044	3/	907	1,179	3/	11,130
Total:						
Average 1950-54	55,220	1,727	9,928	19,493	66,473	152,841
Average 1955-59	79,637	2,007	14,914	21,508	86,324	204,390
1960	87,906	1,778	15,594	18,676	111,734	235,688
1961	95,608	1,576	15,479	20,334	119,685	252,682
1962	84,857	1,219	12,519	17,787	115,316	231,698
1963	83,581	1,042	12,737	19,563	108,002	224,925
1964	86,654	1,219	14,881	20,560	112,244	235,558
1965	83,678	1,571	13,200	18,726	102,432	219,607
1966	75,167	1,483	12,999	18,382	104,996	213,027
1967	72,811	1,502	14,813	17,144	96,220	202,490
1968 2/	76,953	1,508	14,447	15,581	109,848	218,337

1/ Data for Northern Hemisphere countries represent stocks remaining on January 1; estimates for Southern Hemisphere countries include the recently harvested new crop of small grains as well as stocks of old grain on January 1. 2/ Preliminary. 3/ Production small and stocks of minor importance.

Foreign Agricultural Service. Prepared or estimated on the basis of official statistics of foreign governments, other foreign source materials, reports of U.S. Agricultural Attaches and Foreign Service Officer, results of office research, and related information.

Canadian wheat supplies increased 7 percent to 27.3 million tons as early season exports fell sharply behind those of a year earlier. Barley stocks, at 6.3 million tons, were down 4 percent, oats were down 13 percent to 4.5 tons and rye was down 22 percent to 408,000 tons. All three crops were cut sharply by the 1967 drought. Corn stocks were up 19 percent, for a 1.4 million-ton total.

Argentina's stocks of fall grains gained 22 percent to 10.7 million tons, principally because of improved harvests. Wheat supplies were up 29 percent but still 12 percent below 1966 holdings. Barley and rye also rose sharply. Corn stocks were down 16 percent to 1.3 million tons, with heavy exports outweighing increased production.

Australia's grain stocks were reduced to 11.1 million tons, off 31 percent as drought reduced all crops severely. Wheat stocks were down 29 percent from a year earlier to 9.0 million tons; still, they were over the 1966 level. Oats and barley were each down 38 percent to 1.2 million and 907,000 tons, respectively.

UNITED STATES DEPARTMENT OF AGRICULTURE

WASHINGTON, D. C.   20250

Official Business

NOTICE

If you no longer need this publication,
check here [____] return this sheet,
and your name will be dropped from
the mailing list.

If your address should be changed [____]
PRINT or TYPE the new address,
including ZIP CODE, and return the
whole sheet to:

Foreign Agricultural Service, Rm. 5918
U. S. Department of Agriculture
Washington, D. C. 20250

FOREIGN AGRICULTURE CIRCULAR

U.S. DEPARTMENT OF AGRICULTURE
Foreign Agricultural Service   Washington D.C.

GRAIN
FG 5-68
July 1968

RECORD WORLD BARLEY AND OATS

PRODUCTION CONFIRMED

World barley and oats production combined set a record of 151 million
metric tons in 1967, 3 percent over the 147 million-ton record of 1966,
according to information available to the Foreign Agricultural Service.

The world barley crop in 1967 is estimated at 106.3 million tons, 5 percent
above the previous year's high. The total barley acreage of 160.8 million
acres was up 3 percent.

Barley production in North America, totaling 13.7 million tons, was down
11 percent. The Canadian crop at 5.4 million tons was 17 percent below
the good 1966 outturn even though the harvested area was 9 percent larger.
Drought in Saskatchewan, Alberta, and British Colombia sharply reduced the
overall yield. The United States produced 8.1 million tons of barley in
1967, down 6 percent, as acreage declined by 10 percent.

The South American barley crop totaled 1.2 million tons, up 29 percent.
The good crop in Argentina, in contrast to the poor 1966 harvest, accounted
for most of the gain.

Barley production in Europe increased by 14 percent, to a record 45.3 million
tons. The West European crop totaled 37.5 million tons, up 17 percent, as
yield increased 13 percent to 59.9 bushels per acre. Production in the Common
Market countries, at 15.9 million tons, was up 27 percent, mainly a result of
optimum weather conditions and increased fertilizer applications.

BARLEY: Acreage, yield per acre, and production in specified countries, year of harvest, average 1960-64, annual 1966 and 1967 1/

Continent and country	Acreage 2/ Average 1960-64 (1,000 acres)	1966 (1,000 acres)	1967 4/ (1,000 acres)	Yield per acre 3/ Average 1960-64 (Bushels)	1966 (Bushels)	1967 4/ (Bushels)	Production Average 1960-64 (1,000 m.t.)	1966 (1,000 m.t.)	1967 4/ (1,000 m.t.)	1966 (Million bushels)	1967 4/ (Million bushels)
North America:											
Canada	6,058	7,461	8,115	28.4	40.4	30.6	3,743	6,558	5,414	301.2	248.7
U.S.	12,078	10,205	9,188	33.8	38.5	40.3	8,831	8,560	8,061	393.2	370.2
Mexico	572	531	576	13.5	19.7	18.6	169	228	233	10.5	10.7
Total 5/	18,710	18,200	17,880	31.3	38.7	35.2	12,745	15,350	13,710	705.0	629.7
South America:											
Argentina	1,097	1,124	---	22.8	19.8	---	93	438	90	20.1	32.2
Chile	69	124	141	33.2	43.7	43.3	122	118	33	5.4	6.1
Colombia	80	126	151	35.8	34.6	28.6	09	95	94	4.4	4.3
Ecuador	265	264	264	14.9	16.5	18.3	86	95	105	4.4	4.8
Peru	149	432	432	19.0	18.6	19.1	86	175	180	8.0	8.3
Uruguay	120	104	64	13.1	12.4	10.8	34	28	15	1.3	0.7
Total 5/	2,660	2,070	2,235	22.4	21.2	25.1	1,295	955	1,230	43.9	56.5
Europe:											
EEC:											
Belgium	95	96	81	68.9	56.4	75.3	68	86	625	22.3	28.7
France	5,645	6,528	6,820	50.8	52.2	65.5	6,239	7,421	9,724	340.8	446.6
Germany, West	2,735	3,883	3,232	57.6	55.8	67.3	3,433	3,869	4,734	177.7	217.4
Italy	97	442	47	23.6	26.3	30.0	266	253	295	11.6	13.5
Luxembourg	20	30	32	46.2	56.6	64.6	20	37	45	1.7	2.1
Netherlands	227	297	264	75.7	64.4	77.8	374	416	447	19.1	20.5
Total EEC	9,449	10,876	11,176	52.4	52.7	65.2	10,790	12,482	15,870	573.2	728.8
Austria	517	568	573	51.2	57.1	61.9	506	06	772	32.4	35.5
Denmark	2,112	2,748	2,856	70.5	69.5	70.5	3,241	4,159	4,385	191.0	201.4
Finland	560	94	855	31.8	34.5	36.6	87	97	681	27.4	31.3
Greece	456	802	93	25.0	36.6	40.0	248	69	839	29.3	38.5
Ireland	396	462	61	58.2	60.6	62.1	502	60	610	28.0	28.0
Norway	407	44	442	47.7	40.1	50.5	423	65	486	18.6	22.3
Portugal	305	274	267	8.5	8.2	15.1	56	49	88	2.3	4.0
Spain	3,536	3,202	3,707	24.6	31.3	32.6	1,893	2,183	2,632	100.3	120.9
Sweden	933	1,404	1,310	51.6	46.1	34.9	1,049	1,408	1,565	64.7	71.9
Switzerland	79	79	77	60.3	62.2	88.3	99	07	148	4.9	6.8
	4,186	6,130	6,022	64.6	65.4	71.6	5,891	8,723	9,390	400.6	431.3
Total Western Europe 5/	22,935	27,805	28,705	50.4	53.0	59.9	25,155	32,070	37,465	1,473.0	1,720.7
Bulgaria	93	1,028	1,038	37.2	47.5	43.6	643	1,064	986	48.9	45.3
Czechoslovakia	77	05	1,759	43.5	43.3	50.6	1,625	1,608	1,937	73.9	89.0
Germany, East	1,029	1,287	1,186	54.2	54.4	55.8	1,214	1,525	1,440	70.0	66.1
Hungary	1,278	1,211	1,104	34.5	34.7	38.6	960	916	927	42.1	42.6
Poland	74	00	1,594	35.1	38.3	40.3	1,342	1,418	1,400	65.1	64.3
Romania	63	68	618	30.3	36.5	40.1	398	483	540	22.2	24.8
Yugoslavia	892	974	848	27.1	33.6	32.8	527	713	606	32.7	27.8
Total Eastern Europe 5/	8,070	8,515	8,150	38.2	41.7	44.2	6,710	7,730	7,840	355.0	360.1
Total Europe 5/	31,005	36,320	36,855	47.2	50.3	56.4	31,865	39,800	45,305	1,828.0	2,080.8
U.S.S.R. (Eur. and Asia) 6/	41,513	47,937	49,173	17.8	23.0	22.6	16,117	24,000	24,200	1,102.3	1,111.5

Algeria	2,254	—	—	11.6	—	71.3	569	36	1,100	6.2	50.5
	4,254	—	4,465	11.9	—		1,104	506	90	23.2	4.1
Tunisia, Republic	1,310	932	125	4.8	3.9	40.4	138	80	110	3.7	5.1
	133	101	121	49.0	46.4	15.6	142	102	41	4.7	1.9
South Africa, Republic of	82	87		19.7	16.4	11.7	36	31	2,540	1.4	116.7
2/	10,385	7,545	9,935	11.5	10.4		2,590	1,710		78.5	
Cyprus	61	202	202	19.1	15.7	25.0	67	69	110	3.2	5.1
Iran	3,500	3,650	3,650	12.5	12.6	12.8	90	1,000	1,020	45.9	46.9
Iraq	2,695	—	84	15.3	—	19.9	897	90	90	32.2	32.1
Israel	165	121	—	18.0	8.0		65	21	45	1.0	2.1
Syria	1,859	—	—	13.4	—	25.7	542	90	90	6.9	13.8
Turkey	6,816	6,696	6,795	22.3	24.0		3,310	3,500	3,800	160.8	174.5
Afghanistan	862	865	7,065	16.1	19.9	15.9	98	75	2,449	17.2	112.5
India	7,765	6,506	872	16.5	16.8	54.4	2,630	2,377	1,032	109.2	47.4
Japan	1,575	969	2,399	46.5	52.4	36.7	1,593	1,105	96	50.8	88.0
Korea, South	2,00	2,376	456	29.1	39.0	10.4	1,332	2,018	104	92.7	4.8
Pakistan	541	436		11.6	10.1		136	96		4.4	
2/	46,190	41,640	42,460	18.6	19.4	19.9	18,710	17,605	18,400	808.6	845.1
Australia	2,263	2,497	2,150	22.4	25.7	17.3	1,065	1,396	811	64.1	37.2
New Zealand	82	88	99	54.8	64.6	58.9	98	124	127	5.7	5.8
5/	2,345	2,585	2,249	22.8	27.0	19.2	1,163	1,520	938	69.8	43.1
World Total 5/	152,810	156,300	160,810	25.4	29.7	30.4	84,485	100,940	106,330	4,636.1	4,883.7

1/ Years ... to ... of harvests in the Northern Hemisphere. Harvests of ... in Hemisphere countries are combined ... of ... for Southern Hemisphere
Hemisphere which ... follow; thus, the crop harvested in the ... Hemisphere in ... is combined with preliminary ... for Southern Hemisphere
harvests ... begin late in ... and early in 1968. 2/ Figures ... to harvested ... as ... as possible. 3/ Yield per ... calculated from acreage
and production ... shown. 4/ Preliminary. 5/ Esti... totals include allowances for producing ... not shown. 6/ Production estimated.

Foreign Agricultural Service. Prepared or ... on the ... of official ... of ... for foreign governments, other foreign material, reports of U.S.
Agricultural ... and Foreign Service Officers, ... and ...

OATS: Acreage, yield per acre, and production in specified countries, year of harvest,
average 1960-64, 1966 and 1967 1/

Continent and country	Acreage 2/			Yield per acre 3/			Production				
	Average 1960-64	1966	1967 1/	Average 1960-64	1966	1967 1/	Average 1960-64	1966	1967 1/	1966	1967 1/
	1,000 acres	1,000 acres	1,000 acres	Bushels	Bushels	Bushels	1,000 m.t.	1,000 m.t.	1,000 m.t.	Million bushels	Million bushels
North America:											
Canada 5/	7,924	7,924	7,436	42.8	47.3	40.9	6,127	5,778		374.7	304.2
United States	24,148	17,847	15,970	43.9	44.9	49.0	14,496	11,631	11,349	801.3	781.9
Mexico	213	230	190	23.9	24.6	27.2	74	82	75	5.6	5.2
Total 6/	32,285	26,020	23,600	44.2	46.3	47.0	20,700	17,495	16,115	1,205.3	1,110.2
South America:											
Argentina	1,502	1,018		34.3	36.5	---	748	540	575	37.2	39.6
Chile	275	168	232	31.4	47.2	47.2	125	115	159	7.9	11.0
Uruguay	204	227	133	22.0	21.9	17.1	65	72	33	5.0	2.3
Total 6/	1,985	1,415	1,400	32.6	35.5	37.9	940	730	770	50.3	53.0
Europe:											
EEC:											
Belgium	208	226	240	93.6	89.4	103.6	428	293	361	20.2	24.9
France	3,265	3,143	2,523	55.3	65.7	75.3	2,340	2,578	2,758	177.6	190.0
Germany, West	3,243	3,282	3,197	80.8	83.9	93.8	2,340	2,340	2,719	161.2	187.3
Italy	303	287	282	36.1	37.0	43.4	525	477	556	32.9	38.3
Luxembourg	39	33	36	65.9	64.7	96.5	37	31	49	2.1	3.4
Netherlands	245	245	217	103.8	100.4	115.9	425	357	365	24.6	25.1
Total EEC	6,781	6,016	5,894	63.4	69.6	80.0	6,236	6,016	6,807	418.6	469.0
Austria	376	311	296	61.5	72.0	75.6	336	325	336	22.4	23.1
Denmark	472	578	600	101.2	103.0	103.9	693	864	904	59.5	62.3
Finland	1,153	1,183	1,134	50.5	51.3	57.7	846	881	900	60.7	64.9
Greece	311	300	269	33.1	40.0	41.7	150	174	163	12.0	11.2
Ireland	352	243	238	71.6	82.2	88.3	366	290	305	20.0	21.0
Norway	136	101	111	70.4	62.8	76.3	139	92	123	6.3	8.5
Portugal	780	539	656	7.0	8.1	12.7	79	63	121	4.3	8.3
Spain	1,347	1,114	1,196	23.5	25.9	25.5	459	418	443	28.8	30.5
Sweden	1,240	1,139	1,085	70.7	69.8	87.9	1,272	1,154	1,383	79.5	95.4
...	31	25	22	95.6	91.0	97.1	43	33	31	2.2	2.1
Total Western Europe 6/	14,510	12,460	12,515	76.8	63.5	71.2	12,325	11,490	12,940	791.6	891.6

Foreign Agricultural Service. Prepared or estimated on the basis of official statistics for foreign governments, other foreign material, reports of U.S. Agricultural Attaches and Foreign Service Officers, results of office research, and related information.

Bulgaria	373	321	321	30.3	36.5	36.5	164	170	170	11.7	11.7
Czechoslovakia	1,097	961	1,070	54.6	53.5	61.6	870	957	746	65.9	51.4
Germany, East	835	645	717	74.3	75.1	73.0	900	760	703	52.4	48.4
Hungary	245	151	138	34.8	32.8	30.9	124	62	72	4.3	5.0
Poland	3,988	3,504	3,529	46.6	52.4	54.7	2,700	2,665	2,800	192.9	183.6
Romania	447	341	309	28.7	34.3	37.9	186	170	170	11.7	11.7
Yugoslavia	801	791	744	30.1	33.6	33.7	350	386	364	25.1	26.6
Total Eastern Europe 6/	7,790	6,715	6,830	46.8	50.4	53.3	5,295	4,915	5,285	364.0	338.6
Total All Europe 6/	22,300	19,175	19,345	54.4	58.9	64.9	17,620	16,405	18,225	1,255.6	1,130.2
U.S.S.R. (Europe and Asia) 7/	21,050	17,791	17,791	21.5	29.0	26.3	6,559	7,500	6,800	468.5	516.8
Africa:											
No	58	—	35	20.2	—	21.7	17	12	11	0.8	0.8
South Africa, Republic of	509	508	745	15.6	13.3	17.0	115	98	184	12.7	6.8
Total 6/	710	630	860	16.0	13.2	17.2	165	120	215	14.8	8.3
Asia:											
Turkey	1,019	988	988	31.3	31.4	33.1	463	450	475	32.7	31.0
Japan	192	133	113	54.3	52.8	61.6	151	102	101	7.0	7.0
Total 6/	4,850	4,550	4,530	21.3	20.7	21.1	1,500	1,370	1,390	95.8	94.4
Oceania:											
Australia	3,383	4,528	3,500	25.0	29.5	15.0	1,228	1,942	762	52.5	133.8
New Zealand	33	31	35	85.9	77.5	85.6	41	35	30	2.4	2.4
Total 6/	3,416	4,559	3,530	25.6	29.9	15.5	1,269	1,977	792	54.6	136.2
World Total 6/	86,750	74,740	71,060	38.7	42.2	43.0	48,720	45,600	44,310	3,052.7	3,141.6

1/ Years shown refer to years of harvest. Harvests of Northern Hemisphere countries are combined with those of the Southern Hemisphere which immediately follow; thus, the crop harvested in the Northern Hemisphere in 967 is combined with preliminary estimates for Southern Hemisphere harvests which begin late in 967 and end early in 1968. 2/ Figures refer to harvested areas as far as possible. 3/ Yield per acre calculated from acreage and production data shown. 4/ Preliminary. 5/ Production and yield reported in bushels of 34 pounds. 6/ Estimated totals include allowances for producing countries not shown. 7/ Production estimated.

France harvested a 9.7 million-ton barley crop, 31 percent over the previous high in 1966 and 56 percent above the 1960-64 average. West Germany's production was up 22 percent, at 4.7 million tons. The United Kingdom had a record 9.4 million-ton barley crop, up 8 percent as acreage declined slightly.

It is notable that per acre yield of barley for France in 1967 was 29 percent above the 1960-64 5-year average. Similarly, West Germany showed a 17 percent gain, the United Kingdom 11 percent, Spain 33 percent, and Greece 60 percent.

The 1967 barley crop in Eastern Europe totaled 7.8 million tons, little changed from the previous year, with acreage declining 4 percent. Czechoslovakia, the largest barley producer in the area, had a 1.9 million-ton crop, up 20 percent, as yield gained 17 percent. The East European barley yield in 1967 showed a gain of 16 percent over the 1960-64 average. This compares with a 19 percent yield increase in Western Europe in the same period.

Barley production in the Soviet Union in 1967 is estimated at 24.2 million bushels, slightly above 1966, with acreage being 3 percent larger.

The African barley crop is estimated at 2.5 million tons, which represents a return to normal levels following the drought reduced outturns of the previous year. The Asian harvest is placed at 18.4 million tons, up 5 percent. The Turkish production is indicated 9 percent higher and that of India 3 percent higher. Australia's crop was reduced by drought to 811,000 tons, compared with the good 1.4 million-ton crop in 1966.

World oat production in 1967 totaled an estimated 44.3 million tons, 3 percent below the previous year and 9 percent below the 1960-64 average. World acreage totaled 761 million acres, down 4 percent.

North American oat production, at 16.1 million tons, was down 8 percent. Canadian production of 4.7 million tons showed a 19 percent decline, a result of reduced acreage and yield. The U.S. harvested 11.3 million tons, down 2 percent, as acreage declined 11 percent.

The South American oat crop totaled 770,000 tons, up 5 percent. Argentina produced 575,000 tons, versus 540,000 tons in 1966.

The 1967 European oat harvest totaled 18.2 million tons, 11 percent above 1966, mainly on improved yields. West European production gained 13 percent, to 12.9 million tons, counter to a long downward trend. The EEC oat crop totaled 6.8 million tons, for a 12 percent gain. France produced 2.8 million tons, up 7 percent, and West Germany 2.7 million tons, up 16 percent. The United Kingdom crop gained 23 percent to 1.4 million tons. The Netherlands had a remarkable yield of 115.9 bushels per acre. The French oat yield in 1967 was 36 percent above the average in 1960-64. Similar comparative gains were shown by West Germany at 16 percent, Sweden at 24 percent, and by the United Kingdom, Austria, and Ireland all at 23 percent.

East European oat production totaled 5.3 million tons, up 8 percent. The Polish crop is estimated at 2.8 million tons, 5 percent higher, while Czechoslovakia's production, of 957,000 tons, was up 28 percent.

Oat production in the Soviet Union was an estimated 6.8 million tons, 9 percent below 1966, because of reduced yields.

South Africa's oat crop was up sharply at 184,000 tons. Production in Turkey is estimated at 475,000 tons, up 6 percent. Australia's drought-stricken crop of 762,000 tons contrasts with the 1.9 million-ton outturn of 1966.

UNITED STATES DEPARTMENT OF AGRICULTURE

WASHINGTON, D. C.   20250

Official Business

NOTICE

If you no longer need this publication,
check here ⬜ return this sheet,
and your name will be dropped from
the mailing list.

If your address should be changed ⬜
PRINT or TYPE the new address,
including ZIP CODE, and return the
whole sheet to:

Foreign Agricultural Service, Rm. 5918
U. S. Department of Agriculture
Washington, D. C. 20250

RECORD WORLD CORN CROP

IN 1967 CONFIRMED

The 1967 world corn crop is estimated at a record 237 million metric tons, 4 percent over the 1966 record, according to information available to the Foreign Agricultural Service. World corn acreage gained 2.6 percent over the previous year, and average per acre yield 1.6 percent.

North American corn production totaled 132.2 million tons, up 13 percent, as acreage increased 5 percent. The Canadian crop at 1.9 million tons was 12 percent above 1966 with a 9 percent larger area. The United States produced a record 119.9 million tons of corn, 15 percent over the previous 1966 record. The U.S. yield was at a record 78.3 bushels per acre, up 8 percent, and acreage was 6 percent higher. The Mexican crop, at 8.5 million tons, gained 4 percent. Limited moisture cut production in Guatemala and El Salvador, while Honduras showed a recovery from a poor 1966 season.

The South American corn crop is estimated at 22.9 million tons, down 1 percent, as decreases and increases in the two principal producing countries, Argentina and Brazil offset each other. Argentina's production of 6.6 million tons was 18 percent below the good 1966 crop because of drought and high temperatures in mid-season. The Brazilian crop, in the other hand, is placed at a record 13.1 million tons, up 9 percent, principally because of increased acreage, as dry weather checked a prospective yield increase.

Corn crops were generally good in Western Europe, except in France, where drought cut production by 15 percent as compared with 1966. Italian production at 3.8 million tons was 9 percent higher although 3 percent below the 1964 record. Spain had a record outturn of 1.2 million tons, up 6 percent.

CORN: Acreage, yield per acre, and production in specified countries, year of harvest, average 1960-64, annual 1966-67 [1]

Continent and country	Acreage [2]			Yield per acre [3]			Production				
	Average 1960-64	1966	1967 [4]	Average 1960-64	1966	1967 [4]	Average 1960-64	1966	1967 [4]	1966	1967 [4]
	1,000 acres	1,000 acres	1,000 acres	Bushels	Bushels	Bushels	1,000 m.t.	1,000 m.t.	1,000 m.t.	Million bushels	Million bushels
North America:											
Canada	500	807	876	71.0	82.2	84.6	903	1,685	1,882	66.3	74.1
United States ...	59,876	56,933	60,385	62.5	72.3	78.3	94,562	104,581	119,943	4,177.4	4,722.2
Costa Rica	175	150	180	16.9	17.1	17.1	76	65	78	2.6	3.1
El Salvador	448	513	450	17.2	20.5	17.7	196	267	202	10.5	8.0
Guatemala	1,682	1,900	1,847	13.3	16.7	14.7	570	805	690	31.7	27.2
Honduras	959	775	1,013	12.5	14.5	13.8	303	285	355	11.2	14.0
Mexico	15,416	18,533	19,000	15.5	17.4	17.6	6,064	8,200	8,500	322.8	334.6
Nicaragua	353	500	500	13.9	13.9	12.0	124	176	165	6.9	6.5
Panama	213	267	272	13.3	12.4	12.2	72	84	84	3.3	3.3
Total [5]	80,640	81,380	85,500	50.4	56.3	60.1	103,220	116,470	132,180	4,585.2	5,203.7
South America:											
Argentina	7,008	8,525	8,508	28.0	36.9	30.5	4,984	8,00	6,600	314.9	259.8
Brazil	19,308	21,503	22,980	20.6	22.0	22.4	10,112	12,00	13,100	472.4	515.7
Chile	183	227	188	37.9	62.8	62.8	176	362	300	14.3	11.8
Colombia	1,814	1,730	1,952	17.5	18.2	17.1	807	800	850	31.5	33.5
Ecuador	508	519	524	11.7	13.3	13.5	151	175	180	6.9	7.1
Peru	833	865	890	23.2	25.5	26.1	490	560	590	22.0	23.2
Uruguay	563	558	---	10.3	8.4	---	147	117	---	4.7	---
Venezuela	1,058	1,154	1,208	17.2	19.0	19.7	461	557	664	21.9	23.8
Total [5]	32,290	36,290	37,950	21.7	25.9	23.9	17,820	23,100	22,860	909.4	900.0
Europe:											
EEC:											
France	2,229	2,375	2,493	46.4	71.8	58.1	2,625	4,331	3,679	170.5	144.8
Germany, West ...	41	77	104	37.6	64.9	74.2	39	127	196	5.0	7.7
Italy	2,816	2,441	2,513	52.2	56.6	60.0	3,732	3,510	3,830	138.2	150.8
Total EEC [2] ...	5,086	4,893	5,110	49.5	64.1	59.6	6,396	7,968	7,705	313.7	303.3
Austria	130	137	148	61.2	78.9	85.0	202	275	316	10.8	12.4
Greece	461	354	344	24.4	35.9	37.8	286	323	330	12.7	13.0
Portugal	1,208	1,169	1,208	18.3	19.0	18.6	562	565	570	22.2	22.4
Spain	1,139	1,127	1,203	37.2	40.3	40.1	1,075	1,154	1,224	45.4	48.2
Total Western Europe [5]	8,030	7,680	8,020	41.8	52.7	49.8	8,520	10,290	10,150	405.0	399.6
Bulgaria	1,601	1,418	1,404	40.7	61.2	57.7	1,655	2,207	2,058	86.9	81.0
Czechoslovakia ...	876	376	361	39.7	49.8	46.1	509	476	423	18.7	16.7
Hungary	3,226	3,057	3,039	40.3	50.3	38.9	3,304	3,907	3,00	153.8	118.1
Romania	8,305	8,125	8,154	27.4	38.9	32.8	5,784	8,022	6,800	315.8	267.7
Yugoslavia [5] ...	6,118	6,178	6,202	26.4	50.9	46.3	5,664	7,980	7,290	314.2	267.0
Total Eastern Europe [5]	19,760	19,160	19,160	33.7	46.4	40.2	16,920	22,590	19,570	889.3	770.4
Total all Europe [5] ...	27,790	26,840	27,180	36.0	48.2	43.0	25,440	32,880	29,720	1,294.4	1,170.0

- 2 -

U.S.S.R. (Europe and Asia) 6/	15,518	7,907	8,550	24.3	33.9	36.8	9,564	6,800	8,000	267.7	314.9
Africa:											
Morocco	1,122	1,083	1,139	11.4	5.6	8.6	297	154	250	6.1	9.8
United Arab Republic	1,793	1,633	1,682	40.0	56.8	53.8	1,823	2,358	2,300	92.8	90.5
Angola	1,465	--	--	10.9	--	--	407	380	--	15.0	--
Kenya	2,900	3,000	--	18.5	20.7	--	1,360	1,633	1,750	64.3	68.9
Malagasy Republic	247	--	--	14.4	--	--	90	--	--	--	--
Rhodesia, Zambia, and Malawi	2,960	--	--	23.2	--	--	1,748	--	--	--	--
South Africa, Republic of	13,106	14,226	--	15.5	26.7	--	5,147	9,638	5,670	379.4	223.2
Total 5/	35,240	37,400	36,580	17.3	23.0	18.7	15,510	21,860	17,420	860.6	685.8
Asia:											
Turkey	1,689	1,618	1,668	21.4	24.3	25.5	916	1,000	1,080	39.4	42.5
China, Mainland	-	--	--	--	--	--	11,580	--	--	28.3	--
Afghanistan	1,236	--	--	22.5	--	--	707	720	--	28.3	--
Taiwan	43	55	59	29.4	37.2	42.7	32	52	64	2.0	2.5
India	11,200	12,506	13,141	15.5	15.7	16.5	4,402	4,991	5,500	196.5	216.5
Indonesia	7,156	7,873	7,413	15.5	15.0	15.7	2,823	3,005	2,960	118.3	116.5
Japan	100	64	52	40.9	38.9	46.2	104	63	61	2.5	2.4
Pakistan	1,190	1,377	1,511	16.5	16.9	20.7	498	590	795	23.2	31.3
Philippines	4,759	5,355	5,426	10.2	10.5	10.8	1,230	1,435	1,483	56.5	58.4
Thailand	922	--	--	30.7	--	--	720	1,227	1,100	48.3	43.3
Total 5/	53,350	57,500	58,090	17.3	17.8	18.2	23,390	25,990	26,910	1,023.2	1,059.4
Oceania:											
Australia	206	202	209	33.6	36.6	37.3	176	188	198	7.4	7.8
New Zealand	8	7	8	77.8	100.0	91.5	16	18	19	.7	.7
Total 5/	214	209	217	35.3	38.8	39.4	192	206	217	8.1	8.5
World Total 5/	245,040	247,530	254,070	31.4	36.2	36.8	195,140	227,300	237,300	8,948.3	9,342.0

1/ Years shown refer to years of harvest in the Northern Hemisphere. Harvests of Northern Hemisphere countries are combined with those of the Southern Hemisphere which immediately follow; thus, the crop harvested in the Northern Hemisphere in 1967 is combined with preliminary forecasts for the Southern Hemisphere harvest which begins early in 1968. 2/ Figures refer to harvested area as far as possible. 3/ Yield per acre calculated from acreage and production data shown. 4/ Preliminary estimates for Northern Hemisphere countries; for the Southern Hemisphere, preliminary forecasts. 5/ Estimated totals include allowances for producing countries not shown. 6/ Production estimated.

Foreign Agricultural Service. Prepared or estimated on the basis of official statistics of foreign governments, other foreign source materials, reports of U.S. Agricultural Attaches and Foreign Service Officers, results of office research and related information.

UNITED STATES DEPARTMENT OF AGRICULTURE

WASHINGTON, D. C.   20250

Official Business

The East European corn crop, at 19.6 million tons, declined 13 percent
from the good 1966 performance because of late-season dry weather. Production dropped in Yugoslavia, Romania, and Hungary, by 6, 13, and 23
percent respectively.

Corn production in the Soviet Union is estimated at 8.0 million tons, for
an 18 percent increase, supported about equally by larger acreage and
higher yield.

In Africa, corn production fell an estimated 20 percent, to 17.4 million
tons. This was the result of severe drought in the southeastern part
of the continent, in contrast to the unusually good moisture supplies of a
year earlier. The South African crop of 5.7 million tons was 41 percent
below the exceptional harvest of the previous season, but still 10 percent
over the 1960-64 average. In Kenya, corn production continued to expand
under a program of breeding and good technology. The 1967 crop is estimated at 1.8 million tons, up 7 percent for the year.

Asia's corn production gained an estimated 4 percent in 1967 to 26.9
million tons. India, with good growing conditions, produced a record crop
of 5.5 million tons, up 10 percent. Protracted drought in Thailand
resulted in a 10 percent decline in that country's harvest. Corn production
in Indonesia and Philippines was changed little from the previous year.
The Turkish crop is estimated 8 percent higher.

RYE
FG 8-68
September 1968

WORLD RYE EXPORTS

CONTINUE TO DECLINE

The long term trend of world rye exports continued to decline during fiscal year 1967, after a slight gain during 1966. Exports of 482.1 thousand metric tons during 1967 were only about one-fourth of the peak level of 2.2 million tons attained in 1963.

The decline from 1966 amounted to slightly less than 100 thousand tons. Most of the decrease was accounted for by three countries -- Turkey 67,600 tons, Sweden 16,300 tons, and USSR 10,600 tons. Canada, the United States, and West Germany, however, increased their exports during 1967 by 36,300 tons, 18,000 tons and 16,000 tons, respectively.

294026

UNITED STATES DEPARTMENT OF AGRICULTURE

WASHINGTON, D. C. 20250

Official Business

RYE: WORLD EXPORTS BY COUNTRY OF ORIGIN

FISCAL YEARS 1964-65, 1965-66, 1966-67 and PRECEDING 5-YEAR AVERAGE

Country of Origin	1959/60 1963/64 Average	1964-65	1965-66	1966-67 1/
	1,000 M.T.	1,000 M.T.	1,000 M.T.	1,000 M.T.
North America:				
United States ....:	264.7	52.1	97.2	115.2
Canada ....:	132.4	125.3	202.5	238.8
Total - North America ....:	397.1	177.4	299.7	354.0
South America:				
Argentina ....:	57.0	96.1	50.5	-
Total - South America ....:	57.0	96.1	50.5	-
Total - Western Hemisphere ...:	454.1	273.5	350.2	354.0
Europe:				
EEC:				
Belgium-Luxembourg ....:	.6	1.5	3.4	2.0
France ....:	9.5	24.7	20.7	15.1
Germany, West ....:	92.9	1.9	6.9	22.9
Italy ....:	-	-	-	.5
Netherlands ....:	18.2	12.1	3.4	2.2
Total - EEC ....:	121.2	40.2	34.4	42.7
EFTA:				
Austria ....:	1.0	-	-	-
Denmark ....:	33.5	.1	.1	.4
Sweden ....:	30.8	1.2	23.8	7.5
Total - EFTA ....:	65.3	1.3	23.9	7.9
Finland ....:	5.2	-	5.2	-
Total - Western Europe .....:	191.7	41.5	63.5	50.6
Eastern Europe: 2/				
Bulgaria ....:	4.2	-	-	-
Czechoslovakia ....:	21.5	-	-	-
Germany, East ....:	32.3	2.8	1.0	1.0
Hungary ....:	.3	.2	.1	-
Poland ....:	-	.1	1.9	1.5
Romania ....:	18.9	45.0	34.4	25.0
USSR ....:	886.9	93.6	60.6	50.0
Total Eastern Europe ....:	964.1	141.7	98.0	77.5
Total - All Europe ....:	1,155.8	183.2	161.5	128.1
Asia:				
Turkey ....:	8.1	76.8	67.6	-
Total - Asia ....:	8.1	76.8	67.6	-
Oceania:				
Australia ....:	1.5	.1	-	-
Total - Oceania ....:	1.5	.1	-	-
World Total ....:	1,619.5	533.6	579.3	482.1
Equivalent 1,000 bushels .....:	63,756.9	21,006.9	22,806.0	18,979.4

1/ Preliminary.
2/ Based on actual imports by recipient countries, intra-trade on calendar
    year basis, and official estimates by FAO and FAS.

GRAIN
FG 7-68
September 1968

WORLD WHEAT AND FLOUR EXPORTS IN 1966-67

OFF FROM THE PREVIOUS YEAR'S RECORD

World total wheat and flour exports in fiscal year 1967 were 10 percent below the previous year's record. While flour exports showed a modest increase of 0.2 percent, wheat exports declined about 11 percent. Most of the decrease in wheat exports was attributed to reduced imports by Communist Bloc countries.

Wheat. From 1955-56 to 1965-66, the wheat export trend was, with only minor exceptions, steadily upward. Total exports, in fact, more than doubled during this period. During 1966-67, however, world exports declined about 11 percent. Three of the six major wheat exporting countries registered declines in that year as follows: United States (15 percent), Argentina (60 percent), and France (42 percent). Canada's exports remained about the same, while gains were registered by Australia (26 percent) and the USSR (87 percent).

Flour. The wheat flour export trend, from 1955-56 through 1963-64, was also upward. The increase amounted to about 50 percent. Total exports since the record year, fiscal year 1964, have declined about 20 percent. Of the four major flour exporting countries, only France showed an increase in exports (43 percent), since the record year, while the other major exporters registered declines -- U.S. (27 percent), Canada (35 percent), and Australia (48 percent). During 1966-67 a very modest increase in flour exports occurred. The major exporters, however, did not share in this increase, as their total exports were off somewhat. Italy, Spain and the USSR all increased their exports substantially, by 50 percent, 130 percent and 105 percent respectively.

Outlook for fiscal year 1968. Based on preliminary data, total world wheat and flour exports in 1967-68 declined for the second year in a row -- about 5 percent from the previous year. Exports to the Free World held about steady, while those to the Communist Bloc again declined somewhat. Of the major exporters, the United States and France increased their exports from the previous year, those of Australia held about steady, while those of Canada and Argentina were substantially lower.

WHEAT AND WHEAT FLOUR (GRAIN EQUIVALENT): World exports by country of origin
fiscal years 1964-65, 1965-66, 1966-67 and preceding 5-year average

	Wheat grain				Wheat flour (grain equivalent)				Wheat and flour (grain equivalent)			
untry of origin	1959/60-1963/64 Average	1964/65	1965/66	1966/67 1/	1959/60-1963/64 Average	1964/65	1965/66	1966/67 1/	1959/60-1963/64 Average	1964/65	1965/66	1966/67 1/
	1,000 M. T.	1,000 M. T.	1,000 M. T.	1,000 M. T.	1,000 M. T.	1,000 M. T.	1,000 M. T.	1,000 M. T.	1,000 M. T.	1,000 M. T.	1,000 M. T.	1,000 M. T.
ca:												
ates	15,669.3	17,173.1	21,365.3	18,127.4	2,710.1	2,174.3	2,003.5	1,851.0	18,379.4	19,347.4	23,368.8	19,978.4
....	9,163.3	10,978.1	13,820.4	13,899.6	1,014.0	844.4	1,040.6	932.9	10,177.3	11,822.5	14,861.0	14,832.5
....	95.9	405.6	476.6	30.1	--	--	--	--	95.9	405.6	476.6	30.1
North America	24,928.5	28,556.8	35,662.3	32,057.1	3,724.1	3,018.7	3,044.1	2,783.9	28,652.6	31,575.5	38,706.4	34,841.0
ca:												
....	2,191.2	4,254.0	7,844.9	3,090.1	7.5	--	--	--	2,198.7	4,254.0	7,844.9	3,090.1
....	15.4	20.8	142.8	87.2	1.0	--	--	--	16.4	20.8	142.8	87.2
South America	2,206.6	4,274.8	7,987.7	3,177.3	8.5	--	--	--	2,215.1	4,274.8	7,987.7	3,177.3
-Luxembourg	119.1	185.8	199.5	104.1	16.5	28.6	30.4	24.6	135.6	214.4	229.9	128.7
....	1,695.0	3,953.7	4,057.1	2,342.4	458.9	640.8	710.8	678.4	2,153.9	4,594.5	4,767.9	3,020.8
, West	69.4	94.0	167.1	136.4	839.4	574.3	487.4	441.3	908.8	668.3	654.5	577.7
ands	71.7	6.3	12.1	31.1	135.6	262.4	393.9	727.7	207.3	268.7	406.0	758.8
- EEC	18.9	301.4	176.3	126.5	1.3	3.0	8.1	14.1	20.2	304.4	184.4	140.7
	1,974.1	4,541.2	4,612.1	2,740.6	1,451.7	1,509.1	1,630.6	1,886.1	3,425.8	6,050.3	6,242.7	4,626.7
....	27.1	--	--	26.4	--	--	--	--	27.1	--	--	26.4
....	26.4	83.4	31.8	38.3	1.8	1.0	.5	.2	28.2	84.4	32.3	38.5
....	171.3	291.2	227.2	119.2	--	--	--	--	171.3	291.2	227.2	119.2
Kingdom	28.6	2.5	2.7	4.3	10.0	10.9	9.8	11.3	38.6	13.4	12.5	15.4
- EFTA	253.4	377.1	261.7	218.2	10.8	11.9	10.3	11.3	265.2	389.0	272.0	229.5
....	12.3	--	--	--	58.7	24.4	24.9	--	71.0	24.4	24.9	--
....	16.0	--	161.8	597.5	--	--	--	3.1	16.0	--	161.8	600.6
....	57.2	--	--	--	1.3	2.4	--	--	58.5	2.4	--	--
....	16.7	--	--	--	23.7	48.0	33.0	76.0	40.4	48.0	33.0	76.0
Western Europe	2,329.7	4,918.3	5,035.6	3,556.3	1,546.2	1,595.8	1,698.8	1,976.5	3,876.9	6,514.1	6,734.4	5,532.8
ope: 2/												
ovakia	6.9	.7	.8	424.0	--	3.5	--	--	6.9	4.2	.8	424.0
....	13.2	--	--	--	--	--	--	--	13.2	--	--	--
East	67.2	2.1	2.2	5.0	--	--	--	--	67.2	2.1	2.2	5.0
....	43.9	46.4	40.2	48.0	17.5	17.0	17.0	15.0	61.4	63.4	57.2	63.0
....	--	--	--	--	2.7	38.4	8.0	1.0	2.7	38.4	8.0	1.0
....	105.1	28.0	571.0	560.0	--	--	--	--	105.1	28.0	571.0	560.0
....	4,297.9	920.1	2,139.0	3,999.0	150.8	238.5	62.0	127.0	4,448.7	1,158.6	2,201.0	4,126.0
&	38.1	--	--	--	--	--	--	--	38.1	--	--	--
Eastern Europe	4,572.3	997.3	2,753.2	5,036.0	171.0	297.4	84.0	143.0	4,743.3	1,294.7	2,840.2	5,179.0
All Europe	6,902.0	5,915.6	7,788.8	8,592.3	1,717.2	1,893.2	1,785.8	2,119.5	8,620.2	7,808.8	9,574.6	10,711.8
....	4.6	--	--	--	17.2	10.3	--	--	21.8	10.3	--	--
inland)	4.3	--	--	--	--	.1	2.8	--	4.3	.1	2.8	--
....	--	--	--	--	29.9	19.8	19.3	39.4	29.9	19.8	19.3	39.4
....	12.4	.3	--	7.0	--	--	--	--	12.4	.3	--	7.0
....	9.1	--	--	--	--	--	--	--	9.1	--	--	--
....	.1	--	--	--	63.8	79.5	86.4	73.2	63.9	79.5	86.4	73.2
....	.7	.4	.9	--	4.3	2.5	1.5	1.7	5.0	2.9	2.4	1.7
....	1.3	.4	2.0	--	.9	.4	--	--	2.2	.8	2.0	--
....	.3	--	--	--	7.7	--	--	--	8.0	--	--	--
....	1.9	20.6	21.5	13.2	15.2	86.0	101.3	46.7	17.1	106.6	122.8	59.9
....	84.9	190.7	8.2	--	1.0	2.0	--	--	85.9	192.7	8.2	--
....	--	--	--	--	5.5	51.8	38.4	35.0	5.5	51.8	38.4	35.0
....	25.0	--	--	--	--	--	--	--	25.4	--	--	--
Asia	144.6	212.4	32.6	20.2	145.9	252.4	249.7	196.0	290.5	464.8	282.3	216.2
....	.2	5.0	5.0	--	35.6	--	--	--	35.8	5.0	5.0	--
ast Africa	--	--	--	--	.3	--	--	--	.3	--	--	--
....	--	--	--	--	.3	.7	--	--	.3	.7	--	--
e	58.5	--	.5	--	--	--	--	--	58.5	--	.5	--
....	--	--	--	--	.1	1.0	--	--	.1	1.0	--	--
and Nyasaland	1.7	23.2	1.4	--	.1	--	--	32.0	1.8	23.4	1.4	--
....	.4	7.4	--	--	2.3	2.9	--	32.0	2.7	10.3	--	32.0
....	--	--	--	--	20.3	29.5	23.5	23.9	20.3	29.5	23.5	23.9
ab Republic	78.3	90.4	75.0	75.0	13.7	7.5	--	--	92.0	97.9	75.0	75.0
....	.5	.9	2.0	3.0	9.6	10.8	18.0	26.0	10.1	11.7	20.0	29.0
Africa	139.6	126.9	83.9	78.0	82.3	52.6	41.5	81.9	221.9	179.5	125.4	159.9
....	4,714.4	5,706.4	5,156.8	6,508.8	752.5	724.2	493.4	443.4	5,466.9	6,430.6	5,650.2	6,952.2
- Oceania	4,714.4	5,706.4	5,156.8	6,408.8	752.5	724.2	493.4	443.4	5,466.9	6,430.6	5,650.2	6,952.2
....	39,035.7	44,792.2	56,712.1	50,433.7	6,431.5	5,941.1	5,614.5	5,624.7	45,467.2	50,734.0	62,326.6	56,058.4
st - 1,000 bushels	1,434,316	1,645,857	2,083,812	1,853,121	236,317	218,298	206,298	206,672	1,670,633	1,864,155	2,290,110	2,059,793
estern Hemisphere	27,135.1	32,831.6	43,650.0	35,234.4	3,732.6	3,018.7	3,044.1	2,783.9	30,867.7	35,850.3	46,694.1	38,018.3

nary.
on actual imports by recipient countries, intra-trade on calendar year basis, and official estimates by IWC, FAO and FAS.

ORLD RYE EXPORTS

ONTINUE TO DECLINE

he long term trend of world rye exports continued to decline during
iscal year 1967, after a slight gain during 1966. Exports of 482.1
housand metric tons during 1967 were only about one-fourth of
he peak level of 2.2 million tons attained in 1963.

he decline from 1966 amounted to slightly less than 100 thousand
ons. Most of the decrease was accounted for by three countries --
urkey 67,600 tons, Sweden 16,300 tons, and USSR 10,600 tons. Canada,
he United States, and West Germany, however, increased their exports
uring 1967 by 36,300 tons, 18,000 tons and 16,000 tons, respectively.

RYE: WORLD EXPORTS BY COUNTRY OF ORIGIN

FISCAL YEARS 1964-65, 1965-66, 1966-67 and PRECEDING 5-YEAR AVERAGE

Country of Origin	1959/60 1963/64 Average	1964-65	1965-66	1966-67 1/
	1,000 M.T.	1,000 M.T.	1,000 M.T.	1,000 M.T.
North America:				
United States ....:	264.7	52.1	97.2	115.2
Canada ....:	132.4	125.3	202.5	238.8
Total - North America ....:	397.1	177.4	299.7	354.0
South America:				
Argentina ....:	57.0	96.1	50.5	-
Total - South America ....:	57.0	96.1	50.5	-
Total - Western Hemisphere ...:	454.1	273.5	350.2	354.0
Europe:				
EEC:				
Belgium-Luxembourg ....:	.6	1.5	3.4	2.0
France ....:	9.5	24.7	20.7	15.1
Germany, West ....:	92.9	1.9	6.9	22.9
Italy ....:	-	-	-	.5
Netherlands ....:	18.2	12.1	3.4	2.2
Total - EEC ....:	121.2	40.2	34.4	42.7
EFTA:				
Austria ....:	1.0	-	-	-
Denmark ....:	33.5	.1	.1	.4
Sweden ....:	30.8	1.2	23.8	7.5
Total - EFTA ....:	65.3	1.3	23.9	7.9
Finland ....:	5.2	-	5.2	-
Total - Western Europe .....:	191.7	41.5	63.5	50.6
Eastern Europe: 2/				
Bulgaria ....:	4.2	-	-	-
Czechoslovakia ....:	21.5	-	-	-
Germany, East ....:	32.3	2.8	1.0	1.0
Hungary ....:	.3	.2	.1	-
Poland ....:	-	.1	1.9	1.5
Romania ....:	18.9	45.0	34.4	25.0
USSR ....:	886.9	93.6	60.6	50.0
Total Eastern Europe ....:	964.1	141.7	98.0	77.5
Total - All Europe ....:	1,155.8	183.2	161.5	128.1
Asia:				
Turkey ....:	8.1	76.8	67.6	-
Total - Asia ....:	8.1	76.8	67.6	-
Oceania:				
Australia ....:	1.5	.1	-	-
Total - Oceania ....:	1.5	.1	-	-
World Total ....:	1,619.5	533.6	579.3	482.1
Equivalent - 1,000 bushels .....:	63,756.9	21,006.9	22,806.0	18,979.4

1/ Preliminary.
2/ Based on actual imports by recipient countries, intra-trade on calendar
   year basis, and official estimates by FAO and FAS.

JULY 1 GRAIN STOCKS GAIN

SHARPLY IN EXPORTING COUNTRIES

Grain stocks on July 1, 1968 in the United States, Canada, Argentina, and Australia were 15 percent higher than a year earlier according to estimates of the Foreign Agricultural Service. Stocks of wheat, rye, barley, oats, and corn in these 4 principal exporting countries totaled 115.4 million metric tons.

Wheat stocks on July 1 were up 17 percent, largely a result of a large crop in the United States and reduced exports from Canada and Argentina. Rye and barley stocks declined 6 and 4 percent respectively. Stocks of oats were off 19 percent with all countries except the United States showing declines. Corn stocks gained 21 percent, mainly on larger U.S. holdings.

In addition to the five grains included in the total shown for the 4 countries the United States held 9.4 million tons of grain sorghum, up 11 percent; Argentina had 990,000 tons, up 24 percent.

Current levels of stocks along with large world crops of wheat and feedgrains in 1968 should provide overall grain supplies for the 1968-69 marketing year than in 1967-68.

The United States, with a record wheat crop, will have an estimated total supply of 58.1 million tons in 1968-69, 11 percent above last year. Canada with a good crop, will have a wheat supply of approximately 37.7 million tons, about 14 percent higher.

- 2 -

GRAINS: Estimated Stocks in Principal Exporting Countries, July 1, 1950-1968

Country and year	Wheat	Rye	Barley	Oats	Corn	Total
	1,000	1,000	1,000	1,000	1,000	1,000
	M.T.	M.T.	M.T.	M.T.	M.T.	M.T.
United States:						
Average 1950-54 ....:	14,259	202	1,606	3,619	31,903	51,589
Average 1955-59 ....:	28,059	316	3,219	4,582	48,690	84,866
1960 ....:	35,745	266	3,640	3,876	64,061	107,588
1961 ....:	38,410	361	3,318	4,709	71,741	118,539
1962 ....:	35,979	200	2,688	4,010	63,067	105,944
1963 ....:	131,929	1,576	3,181	3,960	54,099	93,945
1964 ....:	21,532	135	2,865	4,534	60,636	92,702
1965 ....:	22,240	326	2,167	4,014	48,094	76,841
1966 ....:	14,565	483	2,281	4,590	45,285	67,204
1967 ....:	11,567	475	2,651	3,923	44,272	62,888
1968 1/ ....:	14,619	462	2,962	3,919	54,585	76,547
Canada:						
Average 1950-54 ....:	9,389	1,356	2,177	2,082	2/	14,004
Average 1955-59 ....:	17,772	432	2,983	2,606	2/	23,793
1960 ....:	17,146	254	3,048	2,005	2/	22,453
1961 ....:	17,554	229	2,830	2,236	2/	22,849
1962 ....:	11,567	152	1,524	1,696	2/	14,939
1963 ....:	14,142	127	2,286	2,776	2/	19,341
1964 ....:	14,560	203	2,939	3,239	2/	20,941
1965 ....:	14,884	224	2,158	2,440	232	19,938
1966 ....:	13,567	287	2,490	2,291	250	18,885
1967 ....:	17,076	245	3,390	2,158	275	23,144
1968 1/ ....:	20,058	210	2,939	1,497	300	25,004
Argentina:						
Average 1950-54 ....:	2,912	406	457	566	2,311	6,652
Average 1955-59 ....:	4,300	483	588	508	3,531	9,410
1960 ....:	3,810	510	480	334	3,556	8,690
1961 ....:	2,722	254	435	580	3,556	7,547
1962 ....:	1,905	254	327	290	3,683	6,459
1963 ....:	2,585	205	305	360	3,175	6,630
1964 ....:	4,763	254	435	435	4,064	9,951
1965 ....:	7,185	230	110	290	3,505	11,320
1966 ....:	2,900	130	140	210	5,200	8,580
1967 ....:	1,570	70	150	160	4,600	6,550
1968 1/ ....:	3,990	70	210	110	4,560	8,940
Australia:						
Average 1950-54 ....:	2,994	2/	196	290	2/	3,480
Average 1955-59 ....:	3,620	2/	370	580	2/	4,570
1960 ....:	3,946	2/	261	653	2/	4,860
1961 ....:	4,082	2/	544	580	2/	5,206
1962 ....:	2,667	2/	327	510	2/	3,504
1963 ....:	4,218	2/	435	510	2/	5,163
1964 ....:	3,184	2/	261	870	2/	4,315
1965 ....:	4,431	2/	333	336	2/	5,100
1966 ....:	3,279	2/	295	550	2/	4,124
1967 ....:	6,627	2/	363	965	2/	7,955
1968 1/ ....:	4,400	2/	181	283	2/	4,864
Total:						
Average 1950-54 ....:	29,554	964	4,436	6,557	34,214	75,725
Average 1955-59 ....:	53,751	1,231	7,160	8,276	52,221	122,639
1960 ....:	60,647	1,030	7,429	6,868	67,617	143,591
1961 ....:	62,768	844	7,127	8,105	75,297	154,141
1962 ....:	52,118	606	4,866	6,506	66,750	130,846
1963 ....:	53,484	508	6,207	7,606	57,274	125,079
1964 ....:	47,039	592	6,500	9,078	64,700	127,909
1965 ....:	48,740	780	4,768	7,080	51,831	113,199
1966 ....:	34,311	900	5,206	7,641	50,735	98,793
1967 ....:	36,840	790	6,554	7,206	49,147	100,537
1968 1/ ....:	43,067	742	6,292	5,809	59,445	115,355

1/ Preliminary. 2/ Production small and remaining stocks believed negligible.

Foreign Agricultural Service. Prepared or estimated on the basis of official statistics of foreign governments, other foreign source materials, reports of U.S. Agricultural Attaches and Foreign Service Officers, results of office research, and related information.

U.S. wheat stocks on July 1, at 14.6 million tons, were up 26 percent, for the first stock increase since 1961. Corn stocks gained 23 percent, to 54.6 million tons; barley was up 12 percent; rye declined 10 percent; and oats were unchanged. U.S. feedgrain stocks, including grain sorghums, totaled 70.9 million tons, 19 percent above a year earlier.

Canadian wheat stocks gained 17 percent, to a record 20.1 million tons. Canadian barley declined 13 percent and oats 31 percent, and rye was 14 percent lower.

In Argentina, July 1 wheat stocks stood at 4.0 million tons in contrast to the low level of a year ago. Only small changes occurred in corn, barley and oats.

Stocks of all Australian grains were down sharply because of drought-shortened crops. Wheat stocks, at 4.4 million tons were off 34 percent. Barley declined 50 percent and oats 71 percent.

UNITED STATES DEPARTMENT OF AGRICULTURE

WASHINGTON, D. C. 20250

_____

Official Business

OREIGN AGRICULTURE CIRCULAR

U.S. DEPARTMENT OF AGRICULTURE
Foreign Agricultural Service   Washington D.C.

GRAIN
FG 10-68
October 1968

WORLD BREADGRAIN PROSPECTS

BETTER THAN 1966 RECORD

World production of breadgrains in 1968 is estimated at 324 million metric tons, on the basis of information available to the Foreign Agricultural Service. This current total harvest of wheat and rye is 5 percent above last year and 3 percent over the previous record of 1966.

World breadgrain area increased 9.5 million acres, 1.6 percent, over the last year and 15.3 million acres compared with 1966. The acreage gain was entirely in wheat, as rye declined in both years.

World wheat production is currently estimated at 294 million tons, 6 percent above the 1967 harvest and 3 percent over the record 285 million-ton crop of 1966. World wheat area continued upward in 1968 and is estimated at 540 million acres, 2 percent over 1967. It is also 4 percent larger than in 1966 and 7 percent above the 1960-64 average.

World wheat yield is estimated at 20.0 bushels per acre, up 4 percent. Plentiful moisture improved growing conditions in Canada and parts of the United States, as compared with last year. Favorable conditions also pertained in northern and western Europe and in much of the spring wheat area of the Soviet Union. Limited moisture supplies have, however, reduced yields variously in countries in an area extending from Austria and Italy in Europe and Syria and Israel in western Asia. On the other hand, unusually good rains produced exceptional harvests in India and Pakistan.

WHEAT: Acreage, yield per acre, and production in specified countries, year of harvest, average 1960-64, annual 1967 and 1968 1/

Continent and country	Acreage 2/ Average 1960-64 (1,000 acres)	Acreage 2/ 1967 (1,000 acres)	Acreage 2/ 1968 3/ (1,000 acres)	Yield per acre Average 1960-64 (Bushels)	Yield per acre 1967 (Bushels)	Yield per acre 1968 2/ (Bushels)	Production Average 1960-64 (1,000 m.t.)	Production 1967 (1,000 m.t.)	Production 1968 3/ (1,000 m.t.)	Production 1967 (in bushels)	Production 1968 4/ (in bushels)
North:											
Canada	26,785	30,121	29,424	20.1	19.7	22.1	11,649	16,137	17,680	592.9	649.6
United States	48,481	59,004	56,039	25.2	25.8	28.5	33,254	41,487	43,053	1,524.3	1,596.6
Mexico	1,971	1,883	1,772	29.4	40.1	37.2	1,577	2,057	1,793	75.6	65.9
Guatemala	83	93	96	10.6	9.5	13.2	24	24	34	.9	1.3
Total 2/	77,325	91,100	87,335	23.5	24.1	26.5	49,705	59,705	62,960	2,193.8	2,313.4
South America:											
Argentina	11,651	14,470	—	22.6	17.8		7,164	7,000	—	257.2	—
Brazil	1,015	890	—	8.6	15.1		238	365	—	13.4	—
Chile	2,090	1,730	—	21.3	25.4		1,213	1,196	—	44.0	—
Colombia	350	68	230	13.0	17.5	20.0	124	80	125	2.9	4.6
Ecuador	46	41	—	13.7	13.7		62	60	—	2.2	—
Peru	377	370	366	14.6	13.9	11.6	150	40	65	5.1	2.4
Uruguay	467	544	370	11.1	17.7	11.5	144	144	120	5.3	1.4
Total 2/	16,995	18,555	18,790	20.4	17.9	20.5	9,095		10,355	332.9	380.5
Europe:											
EEC:											
Belgium	513	492	497	57.1	61.8	56.3	798	828	761	30.4	28.0
France	10,459	9,721	10,208	41.3	54.4	51.6	11,746	13,819	14,340	528.5	526.9
Germany, West	3,430	3,495	3,618	50.7	61.2	61.5	4,731	9,561	6,060	213.4	222.7
Italy	11,000	9,913	10,550	27.6	35.5	32.0	8,261	9,149	9,200	351.4	338.0
Luxembourg	48	38	375	33.9	47.4	66.9	44	11	8	1.8	.3
Netherlands	326	381	375	65.8	71.2		583	739	682	27.1	25.1
Total EEC	25,776	24,040	25,288	37.3	48.0	45.5	26,163	1,045	31,193	1,153.0	1,112.5
Austria	683	782	755	38.3	49.2	42.5	712	874	871	38.1	32.1
Denmark	299	225	230	59.8	68.8	67.2	421	507	421	15.5	15.5
Finland	598	623	—	25.9	29.9		422			18.6	
Greece	2,690	2,315	2,538	23.5	29.3	22.0	1,722	1,848	1,519	67.9	55.8
Ireland	294	189	219	43.9	48.6	48.6	351	255	290	9.4	10.7
Norway	21	8	7	38.0	48.6	42.0	22	11	8	.4	.3
Portugal	1,754	1,680	1,631	11.0	12.4	15.7	526	566	698	20.8	25.6
Spain	10,251	10,549	9,760	11.8	19.5	21.1	4,120	5,598	5,606	205.7	206.0
Sweden	683	628	605	46.1	65.5	61.2	858	1,130	1,008	41.5	37.0
Switzerland	257	255	—	49.0	62.2		343	432		15.9	
Total Western Europe 5/	45,370	43,599	44,325	31.6	39.7	38.5	39,019	47,107	46,100	1,730.8	1,704.9
Albania	283			12.8	44.9		99				
Bulgaria	3,057	2,619	—	25.2	40.0		2,100	3,200	—	117.6	—
Czechoslovakia	1,739	2,296	—	35.5	56.1		1,682	2,500	—	91.9	—
Germany, East	1,027	1,317	—	46.1	36.3		1,288	2,012	—	73.9	—
Hungary	2,594	2,609	—	26.2	33.3		1,849	1,936	—	99.8	—
Poland	3,619	4,344	—	28.2	29.7		2,781	3,934	—	144.5	—
Romania	7,256	7,166	—	19.5	38.1		3,823	5,800	—	213.1	—
Yugoslavia	5,135	4,645	4,942	25.9	36.4	32.5	3,618	4,820	4,370	177.1	160.6
Total Eastern Europe 5/	24,710	25,296	26,235	25.6	32.1	32.5	17,210	25,082	23,100	921.6	848.8
Total Europe 5/	70,080	68,895	70,560	29.5	38.5	36.2	56,259	72,189	69,500	2,652.5	2,553.7
U.S.S.R. (Europe and Asia) 6/	160,000	165,600	—	11.5	14.2	—	50,000	61,000	65,000	2,351.6	—

	Acreage			Yield			Production			Metric	
Africa:											
Algeria	4,733	--	--	10.0	--	--	1,290	--	--	49.6	--
Ethiopia	911	--	--	10.4	--	--	259	--	--	--	--
Morocco	3,905	4,389	4,885	9.7	18.3	--	1,036	1,090	2,411	40.0	88.6
Sudan	47	--	--	23.0	9.1	--	30	86	--	3.2	--
Tunisia	2,661	2,011	--	6.0	5.5	--	86	300	400	11.0	14.7
United Arab Republic	1,440	1,150	--	38.1	38.0	--	432	1,500	--	55.1	--
Kenya	267	372	--	16.2	22.9	--	1,504	232	--	8.5	--
South Africa, Repub lc of	2,851	3,050	--	11.1	12.3	--	117	93	--	37.6	--
Total 5/	17,625	18,115	19,180	11.9	12.1	14.4	5,685	6,080	7,510	223.4	275.9
Asia:											
Cyprus	178	149	--	10.8	23.8	--	52	97	30	3.5	1.1
Iran	4,925	--	--	20.4	--	--	2,740	4,000	4,400	147.0	161.7
Iraq	3,060	--	--	8.7	--	--	726	700	--	25.7	--
Israel	128	222	--	19.5	36.4	28.1	68	220	170	8.1	6.2
Jordan	64	680	--	8.1	12.3	9.4	133	226	173	8.3	6.4
Lebanon	142	150	--	9.8	17.1	11.0	38	70	45	2.4	1.7
Turkey	16,400	17,800	18,000	15.6	18.6	17.6	6,980	9,000	8,600	330.7	316.0
Syria	2,750	--	--	9.7	--	--	728	60	450	22.0	16.5
China, Mainland	62,500	60,500	--	12.7	--	--	21,600	23,000	--	845.0	--
Afghanistan	5,700	--	--	11.0	--	--	2,200	2,550	--	93.7	--
India	33,123	31,172	34,755	11.3	15.6	18.0	10,809	11,528	17,000	423.4	624.6
Japan	1,475	907	795	12.1	13.6	46.7	1,381	310	1,011	36.6	37.1
Korea, South	328	375	389	30.4	30.1	28.4	269	163	301	11.4	11.1
Nepal	330	305	--	15.0	15.0	--	135	163	178	6.0	6.5
Pakistan	12,301	13,385	--	12.1	12.1	15.2	4,065	4,393	6,357	161.4	233.6
Total 5/	144,820	144,660	151,095	13.3	11.8	15.6	52,295	58,290	64,610	2,111.7	2,374.0
Oceania:											
Australia	15,805	22,711	--	19.3	12.2	12.2	8,298	7,548	--	277.3	--
New Zealand	197	308	--	46.3	48.4	48.4	248	405	--	14.9	--
Total 5/	16,002	23,018	--	19.6	12.7	20.4	8,546	7,953	11,020	292.2	515.1
World Total 5/	502,850	530,300	540,300	16.9	19.2	20.0	231,750	277,280	293,960	10,188.2	10,801.1

1/ Years shown ... for harvest in the ... which ... follow; ... harvests ... begin in 1968 ... and early in 1969. 2/ Harvested acreage ... Harvests of the Northern ... for producing ... at 36.74/33. 5/ Estimated totals include ... countries ... in 1968 is combined ... as ... at ... 3/ Preliminary. 4/ Metric ... converted ... estimated ... of the Southern ... for the Southern ... converted

Foreign Agricultural Service. ... of U.S. Agricultural ... Foreign Service ... of foreign governments, ... foreign source ma...

RYE: Acreage, yield per acre and production in specified countries, year of harvest, average 1960-64, annual 1967 and 1968 1/

Continent and country	Acreage 2/ Average 1960-64 1,000 acres	1967 1,000 acres	1968 3/ 1,000 acres	Yield per acre Average 1960-64 Bushels	1967 Bushels	1968 3/ Bushels	Production Average 1960-64 1,000 m.t.	1967 1,000 m.t.	1968 3/ 1,000 m.t.	1967 Million bushels 4/	1968 3/ Million bushels 4/
North America:											
Canada	616	758	679	17.5	17.5	19.6	274	337	337	13.3	13.3
United States	1,699	1,072	1,019	19.2	22.5	23.7	827	612	613	24.1	24.1
Total	2,315	1,830	1,698	18.7	20.4	22.0	1,101	949	950	37.4	37.4
South America:											
Argentina	1,553	--	--	12.0	--	--	474	352	--	13.9	--
Europe:											
EEC:											
Belgium	112	68	67	18.4	52.2	51.7	138	90	88	3.5	3.5
France	620	459	420	23.7	31.0	31.1	373	362	332	14.2	13.1
Germany, West	2,905	2,408	2,377	43.7	51.7	52.0	3,225	3,162	3,141	124.5	123.7
Italy	139	113	99	25.2	28.4	30.2	89	82	76	3.2	3.0
Luxembourg	8	8	--	34.1	49.2	--	7	10	--	.4	--
Netherlands	79	161	106	47.9	52.0	49.7	59	239	235	9.4	9.3
Total EEC	3,863	3,217	3,069	41.4	41.9	40.7	3,891	3,945	3,872	155.2	152.8
Austria	165	342	351	35.4	53.0	39.2	401	397	350	15.6	13.8
Denmark	356	91	91	46.3	51.0	51.0	418	118	118	4.6	4.6
Finland	230	238	--	24.0	26.9	--	140	163	--	6.4	--
Greece	59	27	24	15.9	20.4	14.8	24	14	9	.6	.4
Norway	3	2	3	39.0	45.5	51.0	2	2	3	.1	.1
Portugal	745	613	576	8.6	13.1	14.7	163	204	215	8.0	8.5
Spain	1,157	954	921	13.4	12.7	15.6	393	309	364	12.2	14.3
Sweden	151	151	168	37.8	52.4	47.1	154	198	201	7.8	7.9
Switzerland	37	37	--	54.8	53.7	--	51	68	--	2.5	--
United Kingdom	19	11	11	42.1	43.6	37.9	20	12	11	.5	.4
Total Western Europe 5/	7,292	5,703	5,580	32.1	37.3	37.9	5,953	5,409	5,370	212.9	211.4
Bulgaria	160	100	--	15.6	19.7	--	64	50	--	2.0	--
Czechoslovakia	1,071	793	--	33.5	34.4	--	911	690	--	27.2	--
Germany, East	2,088	1,843	--	33.6	42.4	--	1,784	1,986	--	78.2	--
Hungary	621	519	--	17.3	22.7	--	273	225	--	8.9	--
Poland	11,468	10,625	--	24.1	22.4	--	7,401	7,760	--	305.0	--
Romania	226	210	--	16.5	19.1	--	91	102	--	4.0	--
Yugoslavia	437	341	334	16.6	19.8	18.9	185	171	160	6.7	6.3
Total Eastern Europe 5/	16,228	14,452	14,160	26.0	29.8	29.4	10,717	10,921	10,580	430.3	416.2
Total Europe 5/	23,520	20,155	19,740	27.9	31.9	31.8	16,670	16,340	15,950	643.3	627.9
U.S.S.R. (Europe and Asia) 6/	40,340	30,685	--	13.0	15.4	--	13,330	12,000	--	472.4	--
Asia:											
Turkey	1,560	1,816	1,804	17.0	17.9	17.0	672	825	780	32.5	30.7
World Total 5/	69,620	56,000	55,500	18.3	21.5	21.4	32,350	30,600	30,200	1,204.7	1,188.9

1/ Years shown refer to years of harvest in the Northern Hemisphere. Harvests of Northern Hemisphere countries are combined with those of the Southern Hemisphere which immediately follow; thus, the crop in the Northern Hemisphere in 1968 is combined with preliminary forecasts for the Southern Hemisphere harvests, which begin late in 1968 and end early in 1969. 2/ Harvested acreage as far as possible. 3/ Preliminary. 4/ Metric tons converted to bushels at 39.368. 5/ Estimated totals include allowances for producing countries not shown. 6/ Production estimated.

Foreign Agricultural Service. Prepared or estimated on the basis of official statistics of foreign governments, other foreign source materials, reports of U.S. Agricultural Attaches and Foreign Service Officers, results of office research, and related information.

In <u>North America</u> wheat production totaled 63.0 million tons, up 5 percent, despite area declines in the three main producing countries. The Canadian crop, at 17.7 million tons, is up 10 percent, with a 12 percent improvement in yield. Wet weather and freezing could possibly modify the current crop estimate, which is 21 percent below the 1966 record.

The U.S. wheat crop is estimated at a record 43.5 million tons, 5 percent above last year's previous high, although acreage was reduced by 5 percent. The U.S. yield rose 10 percent to a record 28.5 bushels per acre in response to generally good growing conditions. The previous high yield of 27.5 bushels per acre occurred in 1958. Mexican wheat production is estimated at 1.8 million tons, down 13 percent, reflecting both reduced acreage and yield.

The <u>European</u> wheat harvest is placed at 69.5 million tons, down 4 percent, while area at 70.6 million acres, increased 2 percent. The West European crop totaled 46.4 million tons, 2 percent below 1967, with yield declining 3 percent from last year's exceptional record. Heavy rains have impeded harvest in some areas but damage has been in quality more than quantity.

Production in the Common Market was less than 1 percent below last year's high, although acreage was 5 percent higher. Wheat crops were little changed from last year's high levels in France, Spain, the United Kingdom, and Sweden. West Germany had a record harvest of 6.1 million tons, up 4 percent, from a record 61.5 bushel yield. The Italian crop at 9.2 million tons, was 4 percent lower as drought reduced yields in southern areas. Limited moisture also cut production and yields sharply in Austria and Greece.

The <u>East European</u> wheat crop is estimated at 23.1 million tons, down 8 percent, on 4 percent larger acreage. Yields in the northern countries of the area were near last year's record levels. However, the Yugoslav crop at 4.4 million tons was down 9 percent on record acreage, as drought cut the yield by 15 percent. Yields in Bulgaria, Romania, and Hungary were similarly affected by inadequate rainfall.

Wheat production in the <u>Soviet Union</u> is currently estimated at 65.0 million tons. Although the winter wheat crop was reduced somewhat, mainly by moisture shortage, conditions were generally favorable in much of the spring wheat producing areas and the total crop will apparently be slightly larger than last year.

With good rains in northwestern <u>Africa</u> large wheat harvests resulted from Morocco through Tunisia. Morocco had an exceptional 2.4 million-ton crop.

Wheat yields in the countries of <u>Western Asia</u> were reduced generally by moisture shortage. The Turkish crop at 8.6 million tons was off 6 percent as area increased moderately. With favorable weather Iran produced a 4.4 million-ton crop, up 10 percent. India had exception- ally good rainfall and with improved technology turned out an estimated record 17.0 million tons of wheat, 47 percent above the previous year; acreage at the same time increased 11 percent. Pakistan, similarly, produced a record crop of 6.4 million tons, up 45 percent with area increased by 15 percent.

While it is too early to forecast wheat production in the <u>Southern Hemisphere</u> with certainty, the main producing countries have had plentiful rainfall in contrast to last year; good crops are antici- pated, with harvests beginning generally in November. Argentine acreage planted to wheat was slightly lower, but the prospect is for a harvest considerably improved over last year. Australia has a record planted acreage and, under continuing favorable circumstances, may well exceed the 12.7 million-ton record of 1966.

<u>World rye production</u> in 1968 is estimated at 30.2 million tons, 1 per- cent below the 1967 outturn. World rye acreage, at 55.5 million acres, is also down 1 percent.

The <u>North American</u> rye crop is placed at 950 thousand tons, virtually unchanged, although acreage declined 7 percent. The Canadian rye crop is reported at 337 thousand tons, unchanged from 1967, while a 10 percent decline in area was compensated by improved yield. U.S. rye production, at 613 thousand tons, is barely over that of last year. Acreage declined 5 percent and yield was up by 5 percent.

<u>European</u> rye production is estimated at 16.0 million tons, down 2 percent, as acreage also declined 2 percent. The <u>Western European</u> harvest is placed at 5.4 million tons, 1 percent below last year. Rye area was down 2 per- cent and yield showed a slight gain over the high 1967 level. The West German crop at 3.1 million tons was 1 percent lower, even though yield gained slightly. French production and area declined by 8 percent. The Spanish outturn was up 18 percent on sharply improved yield.

Rye production in <u>Eastern Europe</u> is estimated at 10.6 million tons, down 3 percent, with area also estimated 3 percent lower. Crops in Poland, East Germany, and Czechoslovakia, the principal producers in the region, are reported near the level of last year. The Soviet Union's rye crop is currently expected to be little changed from 1967.

Turkish rye production is placed at 780 thousand tons, down 4 percent. The South American rye harvest is expected to be higher because of im- proved moisture supplies.

UNITED STATES DEPARTMENT OF AGRICULTURE

WASHINGTON, D. C. 20250

Official Business

FOREIGN AGRICULTURE CIRCULAR

U.S. DEPARTMENT OF AGRICULTURE
Foreign Agricultural Service   Washington D.C.

GRAIN
FG 11-68
October 1968

WORLD FEEDGRAIN EXPORTS DOWN

THREE PERCENT IN FY 1967 BUT

47 PERCENT ABOVE AVERAGE

World feedgrain exports, during fiscal year 1967, declined slightly
from the previous year, but exceeded the five year average (1960-64)
by about 47 percent. Declines in exports of corn, barley, and oats
(2,170, 575, and 335 thousand metric tons, respectively) as compared
with the previous year were partially offset by increased shipments
of grain sorghum.

The Western Hemisphere continued as the major supplier of feedgrains.
The United States remained the dominant single supplier providing 49
percent of the total, while Argentina retained second place supplying
15 pereent. France's market share was 9 percent, while the USSR,
Thailand, United Kingdom, Canada, and Mexico each had from 2.5 to 3.0
percent of the total.

Although total world corn exports were about 10 million tons above
the five year average, 1967 exports were down nearly 10 percent from
a-year earlier. A drop in United States exports of 3.5 million tons
during 1967 was partially offset by gains in Argentina (2.2 million
tons) and France (1.1 million tons). Total shipments from other
exporters registered a net decline.

The long term trend of increasing grain sorghum exports continued
during 1967. The increase amounted to 23 percent. Significant
increases were registered by the United States (923 thousand tons),
Argentina (726 thousand tons), France (45 thousand tons), and Thailand
(38 thousand tons), while those of South Africa declined 36 thousand
tons.

FEED GRAIN: World exports by country of origin, fiscal years 1964-65, 1965-66, 1966-67 and preceding 5-year average.

Country of origin	Corn 1959/60-1963/64 Average 1,000 M.T.	Corn 1964/65 1,000 M.T.	Corn 1965/66 1,000 M.T.	Corn 1966/67 1/ 1,000 M.T.	Grain Sorghum 1959/60-1963/64 Average 1,000 M.T.	Grain Sorghum 1964/65 1,000 M.T.	Grain Sorghum 1965/66 1,000 M.T.	Grain Sorghum 1966/67 1/ 1,000 M.T.	Oats 1959/60-1963/64 Average 1,000 M.T.	Oats 1964/65 1,000 M.T.
North America:										
United States	8,745.1	13,079.9	15,988.2	12,551.6	2,493.3	3,018.2	6,177.4	7,100.6	1,692.4	59.9
Canada	2.3	7.1	8.8	2.2	1.9	23.0	5.7	3.9	160.4	189.7
Mexico	92.2	945.0	1,327.4	1,406.4				20.9		
Total - North America	8,839.6	14,032.0	17,324.4	13,960.2	2,494.5	3,041.6	6,183.1	7,125.4	1,853.0	250.2
Central America:										
Costa Rica	2.1	.2	--	--						
El Salvador	1.6	1.8	2.9	1.5	1.1	.8	2.5	.3		
Guatemala	1.1	--	--	5.6	.4	.7	1.0	.2		
Honduras	22.4	73.7	55.7	22.4	.1	.1				
Nicaragua	--	--	.7	.6						
Total - Central America	27.6	75.7	59.7	30.1	1.6	2.6	3.5	.5		
Bermuda and Caribbean:										
Bermuda	--	--	--	--						
Dominican Republic	11.9	--	2.8	.5						
Total - Bermuda and Caribbean	11.9	--	2.8	2.2						
South America:										
Argentina	2,499.0	3,442.4	2,922.9	5,082.3	441.7	706.8	512.7	1,238.7	255.3	490.8
Brazil	155.2	26.2	635.2	3,598.7	.2	5.9	3.8	2.5		
Chile	--	1.0	--	--					.1	1.4
Colombia	--	--	--	--						
Guyana	--	--	--	.4						
Paraguay	10.5	10.4	4.8	1.4						
Peru	.5	.9	1.2	1.6						
Uruguay	--	--	--	--						
Total - South America	2,665.2	3,480.9	3,564.1	8,684.4	441.9	712.7	516.5	1,241.2	255.4	492.2
Total - Western Hemisphere	11,544.3	17,588.6	21,855.0	22,910.0	2,940.6	3,756.9	6,703.1	8,367.1	2,108.4	742.5
Europe:										
EEC:										
Belgium and Luxembourg	34.5	62.1	115.6	120.2	17.7	7.8	58.1	94.4	1.4	1.4
France	413.4	551.2	879.1	1,835.6	1.6	13.7	28.9	74.0	20.7	29.6
Germany, West	31.7	293.1	333.3	115.9	4.9	34.6	19.0	23.4	18.4	42.6
Italy	33.7	468.2	505.3	75.8	2.9	3.7	2.8	2.5		
Netherlands	46.6	65.5	28.8	8.1	17.6	33.3	13.9	6.5	2.7	1.9
Total - EEC	599.9	1,440.1	1,892.1	2,155.6	44.7	93.1	122.7	200.8	43.2	109.3
EFTA:										
Austria	1.6	1.8	.3	1.7	.2	.3	.4	.7	22.3	26.4
Denmark	.6	.8	.4	--					5.6	
Norway	--	--	--	--						
Portugal	.1	--	--	--						
Sweden	--	--	--	--					59.3	128.3
Switzerland	--	1.1	.4	--						
United Kingdom	--	--	--	--					21.2	1.2
Total - EFTA	2.3	3.7	1.1	1.7	.2	.3	.4	.7	108.4	155.9
Cyprus	--	--	--	--						
Finland	--	--	--	--					3.1	
Ireland	--	--	--	--					1.0	.3
Spain	--	--	--	--	7.8					
Total - Western Europe	562.2	1,443.9	1,893.2	2,157.3	52.7	93.7	124.3	202.0	155.7	339.2
Eastern Europe: 2/										
Albania	.2	--	--	--						
Bulgaria	80.8	144.2	75.0	100.0	.2		.5			
Czechoslovakia	8.4	38.2	35.0	--						
Germany, East	1.8	--	--	--						
Hungary	39.4	78.2	67.6	50.0	1.0	.7	.4	.3	.4	
Poland	1.1	1.8	--	--						
Romania	594.8	650.0	350.0	300.0	4.6	2.8	1.8	1.7	.3	
U.S.S.R.	557.4	744.1	650.0	575.0					80.0	20.1
Yugoslavia	267.7	311.0	202.6	500.0	1.9	.5	.7	1.0	4.3	
Total - Eastern Europe	1,551.5	1,969.5	1,380.2	1,525.0	8.0	4.1	3.1	3.3	85.0	20.1
Total - All Europe	2,113.8	3,413.4	3,233.8	3,682.3	60.3	97.9	128.4	205.3	240.7	359.3

FEED GRAIN: World exports by country of origin, fiscal years 1964-65, 1965-66, 1966-67 and preceding 5-year average

All figures in 1,000 M.T.

Country of origin	Oats 1965/66	Oats 1966/67 1/	Barley 1959/60-1963/64 average	Barley 1964/65	Barley 1965/66	Barley 1966/67 1/	Total Feed Grains 1959/60-1963/64 average	Total Feed Grains 1964/65	Total Feed Grains 1965/66	Total Feed Grains 1966/67 1/
North America:										
United States	523.6	246.7	1,819.4	1,263.0	1,618.4	936.2	14,750.2	17,421.0	25,307.6	20,831.1
Canada	276.2	79.0	821.3	723.0	706.4	991.8	985.9	942.8	997.1	1,076.9
Mexico	---	---	---	---	---	---	92.9	946.1	1,327.4	1,067.3
Total - North America	799.8	321.7	2,640.7	1,986.0	2,324.8	1,928.0	15,829.0	19,309.9	27,632.1	22,978.1
Central America:										
Costa Rica	---	---	---	---	---	---	2.1	.2	---	---
El Salvador	---	---	---	---	---	---	2.2	2.6	2.9	1.5
Guatemala	---	---	---	---	---	---	1.7	1.7	3.2	5.9
Honduras	---	---	---	---	---	---	22.6	74.8	56.4	22.6
Nicaragua	---	---	---	---	---	---	.6	---	.7	.6
Total - Central America	---	---	---	---	---	---	29.4	78.3	63.2	30.6
Bermuda and Caribbean:										
Bermuda	---	---	---	---	---	---	---	---	---	.5
Dominican Republic	---	---	---	---	---	---	11.9	11.9	2.8	2.2
Total - Bermuda and Caribbean	---	---	---	---	---	---	11.9	11.9	2.8	2.7
South America:										
Argentina	167.1	157.7	196.2	445.8	445.3	50.8	3,392.4	5,095.8	3,748.0	6,529.5
Brazil	---	---	---	---	---	---	156.4	32.1	639.0	602.2
Chile	.8	.5	2.7	1.5	8.5	7.0	2.8	2.9	9.3	7.5
Colombia	---	---	---	---	---	---	---	1.0	---	---
Guyana	---	---	---	---	---	---	---	---	---	---
Paraguay	---	---	---	---	---	---	10.5	10.4	4.8	.4
Peru	---	---	---	---	---	---	.5	.9	1.2	1.4
Uruguay	---	---	3.3	---	4.5	5.4	3.3	---	.5	.6
Total - South America	167.9	158.2	202.2	447.3	458.3	63.2	3,565.9	5,133.1	4,406.8	7,146.0
Total - Western Hemisphere	967.7	480.9	2,842.9	2,433.3	2,783.1	1,991.2	19,436.2	24,521.5	32,104.9	30,157.3
Europe:										
EEC:										
Belgium and Luxembourg	.8	2.0	7.0	29.4	56.1	52.5	60.6	100.7	230.6	269.1
France	41.2	44.3	1,284.2	2,240.5	1,839.4	1,838.3	1,719.9	2,835.0	2,786.6	3,792.2
Germany, West	61.5	32.4	44.9	43.5	38.3	20.2	96.9	413.8	442.1	191.9
Italy	6.7	.1	---	4.2	4.2	---	36.6	112.0	55.9	78.4
Netherlands	87.8	117.4	147.0	146.0	164.3	151.0	206.9	351.1	299.8	283.0
Total - EEC	198.0	196.2	1,473.0	2,459.4	2,102.3	2,062.0	2,120.9	3,812.6	3,815.0	4,614.6
EFTA:										
Austria	---	---	1.0	.1	---	---	2.6	1.9	.3	1.7
Denmark	17.1	12.0	86.6	222.0	280.2	223.7	11.7	249.5	298.1	236.4
Norway	4.2	---	4.2	---	---	---	9.8	---	---	---
Portugal	---	---	---	---	---	---	120.8	247.6	212.3	218.9
Sweden	123.5	134.9	61.5	119.3	88.4	84.0	---	---	---	---
Switzerland	---	---	---	---	---	---	---	---	---	---
United Kingdom	.5	.1	217.4	112.2	678.1	1,108.5	246.4	113.5	679.7	1,109.1
Total - EFTA	145.3	147.0	372.7	453.7	1,046.7	1,416.2	491.0	613.7	1,490.5	1,566.1
Cyprus	---	---	5.7	23.8	76.3	15.0	5.7	23.0	76.3	15.0
Finland	---	---	6.4	---	---	---	6.4	---	---	---
Ireland	---	---	24.7	.1	.1	---	25.7	.4	.1	---
Spain	---	---	---	---	---	---	.3	---	---	.7
Total - Western Europe	339.1	343.2	1,879.5	2,937.0	3,225.4	3,493.9	2,650.1	4,813.8	5,402.0	6,196.4
Eastern Europe 2/:										
Albania	---	---	---	---	---	---	---	---	---	---
Bulgaria	---	---	.3	---	2.3	1.5	84.2	114.2	77.8	101.5
Czechoslovakia	---	---	205.8	218.5	244.5	250.0	244.2	256.7	276.5	250.0
Germany, East	---	---	11.5	38.2	19.9	5.0	13.7	38.2	19.9	5.0
Hungary	---	---	6.9	---	5.0	---	47.3	78.9	68.0	50.3
Poland	---	---	62.1	58.4	73.4	74.8	63.6	74.5	74.5	75.1
Romania	.9	10.0	502.7	1,366.8	60.0	750.0	601.8	652.8	352.7	301.7
U.S.S.R.	15.0	12.0	111.0	1,340.1	1,655.5	88.4	681.1	1,340.1	1,655.5	1,335.0
Yugoslavia	---	---	58.9	---	89.4	88.4	280.1	58.9	255.5	595.4
Total - Eastern Europe	17.3	17.3	801.1	1,707.3	1,397.9	1,159.7	2,015.8	2,645.0	2,799.5	2,710.0
Total - All Europe	356.4	355.2	2,680.6	4,644.3	4,623.3	4,653.6	5,095.9	7,458.8	8,234.9	8,906.4

- 3 -

FEED GRAIN: World exports by country of origin, fiscal years 1964-65, 1965-66, 1966-67 and preceding 5-year average - Continued

Country of origin	Corn				Grain Sorghum				Oats	
	1959/60-1963/64 Average 1,000 M.T.	1964/65 1,000 M.T.	1965/66 1,000 M.T.	1966/67 1/ 1,000 M.T.	1959/60-1963/64 Average 1,000 M.T.	1964/65 1,000 M.T.	1965/66 1,000 M.T.	1966/67 1/ 1,000 M.T.	1959/60-1963/64 Average 1,000 M.T.	1964/65 1,000 M.T.
Asia:										
Aden	---	---	---	---	7.0	8.1	5.6	3.0	---	---
Burma	20.2	19.5	10.0	5.0	---	---	---	---	---	---
Cambodia	125.2	150.8	90.0	50.0	---	---	---	---	---	---
China (Mainland)	38.8	285.0	162.1	125.0	13.4	---	10.6	10.0	---	---
Hong Kong	4.3	.4	.4	.1	---	---	---	---	---	---
Indonesia	---	---	5.7	127.3	---	---	---	---	---	---
Iran	---	---	---	---	---	---	---	---	---	---
Iraq	1.1	---	---	---	.6	---	1.2	.5	---	---
Israel	---	---	---	---	.2	---	.1	---	.1	---
Japan	---	---	1.0	---	---	---	---	---	---	---
Jordan	15.8	1.6	---	2.5	---	1.1	1.4	.2	---	---
Korea, North	2.5	---	10.2	1.0	---	---	2.0	4.2	---	---
Korea, South	.4	2.1	1.2	.5	---	---	---	---	---	---
Lebanon	7.2	---	---	---	---	---	---	---	---	---
Malaysia	4.3	16.5	31.3	20.6	---	---	---	---	---	---
Singapore	2.0	2.2	2.4	2.0	5.2	6.6	10.0	4.5	---	---
Syria	---	---	---	.6	---	---	.1	.6	---	---
Taiwan	606.5	896.5	1,132.3	1,096.0	.2	12.5	85.7	123.9	---	---
Thailand	1.1	---	---	---	3.9	11.5	5.3	13.2	3.0	---
Turkey	2.2	---	---	---	---	---	---	---	---	---
Vietnam, North										
Total - Asia	830.5	1,370.4	1,446.8	1,430.7	30.5	39.8	122.0	160.1	3.1	---
Africa:										
Algeria	.7	---	---	---	.2	.2	.2	.2	2.7	---
Angola	121.3	152.6	133.6	69.5	---	---	---	---	---	---
Burundi and Rwanda	---	---	---	---	---	---	---	---	---	---
Congo (Leopoldville)	1.2	---	---	---	---	---	---	---	---	---
Ghana	---	.1	.2	.2	---	.2	.2	.2	---	---
Kenya	43.8	2.3	2.5	1.0	.9	10.2	25.3	19.7	4.9	1.7
Malagasy	3.4	.6	.6	.4	---	---	---	---	---	---
Morocco	60.9	60.9	25.6	83.7	34.9	---	---	---	---	---
Mozambique	2.5	9.3	.1	.1	1.7	29.8	.6	---	---	---
Niger	---	---	---	---	---	---	---	---	---	---
Nigeria	2.2	.2	.1	5.0	1.7	.9	.5	.3	.3	---
Portuguese Guinea	189.2	15.7	10.0	482.4	---	---	---	---	---	---
Rhodesia and Nyasaland	1,590.8	673.3	479.6	---	67.7	99.3	161.4	125.4	3.6	---
Rwanda	---	---	---	---	---	---	---	---	---	---
South Africa	---	---	---	---	98.2	50.5	126.3	28.4	---	---
Sudan	.9	29.8	2.0	.2	2.2	1.9	2.0	---	---	---
Tanganyika	10.7	---	.6	27.9	.3	---	---	---	1.1	---
Tunisia	---	---	---	---	---	---	---	---	---	---
Uganda	2.9	1.8	1.0	14.8	---	---	---	---	---	---
United Arab	1.0	.2	---	---	.4	.2	.5	---	---	---
Zambia	---	---	---	---	---	---	---	---	---	---
Zanzibar	.3	---	---	---	.1	---	---	.1	---	---
Total - Africa	2,031.8	946.8	655.2	635.2	208.4	193.0	316.9	174.0	12.3	2.4
Oceania:										
Australia	2.2	.5		2.0	32.0	14.0	4.3	42.8	322.5	366.8
Total - Oceania	2.2	.5		2.0	32.0	14.0	4.3	42.8	322.5	366.8
World Total	16,522.6	23,043.7	27,286.6	25,117.6	3,272.3	4,101.6	7,274.7	8,949.3	2,687.0	1,471.0
Equivalent - 1,000 Bushels	650,459	907,181	1,074,223	988,826	128,823	161,471	286,389	352,315	185,118	101,343

1/ Preliminary.
2/ Based on actual imports by recipient countries, intra-trade on calendar year basis, and official estimates by FAO and FAS.

1,000 M.T.	1,000 M.T.	1,000 M.T.	1,000 M.T.	1,000 M.T.	1,000 M.T.	1,000 M.T.	1,000 M.T.	1,000 M.T.	1,000 M.T.	
										:Asia:
--	--	--	--	--	--	7.0	8.1	5.6	3.0	: Aden
--	--	--	--	--	--	20.2	19.5	10.0	5.0	: Burma
--	--	--	--	--	--	125.2	150.8	90.0	50.0	: Cambodia
--	--	.4	--	.5	.5	57.5	285.4	173.5	135.5	: China (Mainland)
--	--	5.3	--	--	--	4.3	5.7	5.7	--	: Hong Kong
--	--	.2	1.2	.3	1.6	.2	1.2	140.8	127.1	: Indonesia
.4	--	--	--	--	1.6	--	--	1.0	1.6	: Iran
--	--	88.5	53.1	139.6	19.0	89.1	53.1	.6	19.5	: Iraq
--	--	--	5.1	.5	.7	.6	1.0	.4	--	: Israel
1.0	--	1.0	.2	.4	--	1.0	.6	11.6	.7	: Japan
--	--	--	--	--	--	15.8	5.1	2.2	--	: Jordan
--	--	--	--	--	--	2.5	1.6	11.0	2.7	: Korea, North
--	--	5.9	3.0	10.0	6.0	6.3	5.1	.2	4.3	: Korea, South
--	--	--	--	--	--	7.2	.2	--	7.0	: Lebanon
--	--	--	--	--	--	4.3	16.5	--	.5	: Malaysia
--	--	130.7	180.9	201.6	15.0	-7.9	189.7	31.3	20.6	: Singapore
--	--	42.3	25.0	--	--	606.7	909.0	244.0	21.6	: Syria
--	--	--	--	--	--	--	--	1,218.0	1.2	: Taiwan
--	--	--	--	--	--	50.3	36.5	--	1,219.9	: Thailand
--	--	--	--	--	--	2.2	5.3	5.3	13.2	: Vietnam, North
--	--	274.0	268.9	353.2	42.8	1,138.1	1,683.1	1,922.0	1,633.6	: Total - Asia
										:Africa:
.1	--	.1	90.0	.4	.2	3.7	90.0	133.6	69.5	: Algeria
--	--	.1	.5	--	--	121.3	152.6	.4	.2	: Angola
--	--	--	--	--	--	.1	.5	--	--	: Burundi and Rwanda
--	--	--	--	--	--	1.2	--	--	--	: Congo (Leopoldville)
--	--	--	--	--	--	44.7	2.5	.4	.4	: Ghana
1.9	1.5	54.1	27.1	3.8	--	.6	.6	2.5	1.0	: Kenya
--	--	--	--	--	--	154.8	99.9	56.6	21.6	: Madagascar
--	--	--	--	--	--	2.5	9.3	.6	83.7	: Morocco
--	--	--	--	--	--	1.7	29.8	.1	--	: Mozambique
--	--	--	--	--	--	--	.2	--	.1	: Niger
--	--	--	--	--	--	2.2	--	--	--	: Nigeria
.7	.3	--	--	--	--	190.9	16.6	10.5	5.3	: Portuguese Guinea
--	--	--	--	--	.1	--	--	--	--	: Rhodesia and Nyasaland
--	--	--	5.5	.2	--	1,662.1	778.1	641.9	608.2	: Rwanda
--	--	--	--	--	--	99.1	50.5	126.3	28.4	: South Africa
--	--	--	--	--	--	31.7	--	--	--	: Sudan
--	--	28.9	1.7	5.0	2.0	12.9	2.4	4.0	.2	: Tanganyika
--	--	--	.5	1.0	2.5	30.3	.3	5.0	28.4	: Tunisia
--	--	1.2	10.0	5.0	1.0	2.9	10.4	1.6	2.0	: Uganda
--	--	--	--	--	--	2.6	--	6.5	11.8	: United Arab Republic
--	--	--	--	--	--	.4	--	--	--	: Zambia
										: Zanzibar
2.5	1.8	304.4	135.3	15.4	3.8	2,336.9	1,277.5	990.1	865.8	: Total - Africa
										:Oceania:
250.8	402.8	553.5	351.6	226.7	421.4	910.2	732.9	481.8	872.0	: Australia
250.8	402.8	553.5	351.6	226.7	421.4	910.2	732.9	481.8	872.0	: Total - Oceania
1,577.5	1,212.7	6,435.4	7,833.4	7,701.7	7,125.8	28,917.3	36,449.7	43,840.7	42,435.4	:World Total
108,680	85,614	295,573	359,782	353,733	321,282					:Equivalent - 1,000 Bushels

1/ Preliminary.
2/ Based on actual imports by recipient countries, intra-trade on calendar year basis, and official estimates by FAO and FAS.

The long term trend in <u>oats</u> exports continued downward. During 1967, exports were less than 50 percent of the 5 year average and were off 8 percent from 1966. Declines in exports were registered by all of the major oat exporting countries.

<u>Barley</u> exports have declined during the past three years, but 1967 exports were still 11 percent above the recent 5 year average. Most of the decline in 1967, compared with the previous year, was registered by the United States (682 thousand tons) and the USSR (250 thousand tons). The United Kingdom and Canada, however, increased exports by 430 thousand tons and 285 thousand tons, respectively.

UNITED STATES DEPARTMENT OF AGRICULTURE

WASHINGTON, D. C. 20250

Official Business

GRAIN
FG 12-68
December 1968

WORLD BARLEY AND OAT PRODUCTION

FORECAST AT NEW RECORD

World production of barley and oats in 1968 is estimated at 157.6 million
metric tons, 5 percent over the previous record of 1967 and 18 percent
above the 1960-64 average, according to the Foreign Agricultural Service.
More plentiful rainfall in Canada and the United States, along with good
growing conditions in northern and western parts of Europe, were largely
responsible for the large total crop.

World barley production in 1968 is estimated at 107.2 million tons, up 4
percent from the 1967 previous record, as barley acreage gained 3 percent.

North American barley production totaled 16.3 million tons, 19 percent
above last year, with acreage and yield contributing about equally to
the gain. The Canadian barley crop, at a record 6.9 million tons was
27 percent larger than last year's short crop, as acreage gained 9
percent. Wet harvest conditions may reduce the current Canadian estimate. The U.S. barley harvest is placed at 9.2 million tons, 15 percent above 1967 and 5 percent over the 1960-64 average. The U.S. acreage
was 9 percent higher and yield rose 5 percent to a record 42.5 bushels
per acre.

The European barley crop totaled 45.0 million tons, down 2 percent. The
West European crop was 37.3 million tons, little changed from last year's
excellent outturn, although acreage was 5 percent greater. The Common
Market harvest totaled 15.1 million tons, down 5 percent on about the
same area. The French crop, at 8.9 million tons, was down 9 percent.
The U.K. harvest is indicated 6 percent lower, at 8.8 million tons,
although poor harvest weather may reduce the outturn further. Denmark
produced a record 5.1 million-ton barley crop, up 15 percent as yield
gained 7 percent. The Spanish crop was up 35 percent to 3.5 million
tons on a commensurate increase in area. Production in Greece was off
sharply because of drought.

OATS: Acreage, yield per acre, and production in specified countries, year of harvest,
average 1960-64, annual 1967 and 1968 1/

Continent and country	Acreage 2/			Yield per acre 3/			Production				
	Average 1960-64	1967	1968 4/	Average 1960-64	1967	1968 4/	Average 1960-64	1967	1968 4/	1967	1968 4/
	1,000 acres	1,000 acres	1,000 acres	Bushels	Bushels	Bushels	1000 m.t.	1,000 m.t.	1,000 m.t.	Million bushels	Million bushels
North America:											
Canada 5/	9,210	7,436	7,766	42.8	40.9	46.1	6,070	4,690	5,515	304.2	357.6
United States	22,784	15,970	17,765	43.9	49.0	52.6	14,496	11,349	13,563	781.9	934.4
Mexico	115	126	136	15.0	15.9	15.2	25	29	30	2.0	2.1
Total 6/	32,110	23,535	25,670	44.2	47.0	51.3	20,600	16,070	19,110	1,107.1	1,316.6
South America:											
Argentina	1,502	1,275	---	34.3	37.3	---	748	690	---	47.5	---
Chile	275	267	---	31.4	47.2	---	125	183	---	12.6	---
Uruguay	208	133	---	17.1	17.3	---	65	33	---	2.3	---
Total 6/	1,985	1,680	1,680	32.6	37.3	---	940	910	---	62.7	---
Europe:											
EEC:											
Belgium	308	240	215	93.6	103.6	92.0	418	361	287	24.9	19.8
France	3,265	2,518	2,325	55.3	75.5	73.3	2,620	2,758	2,472	190.0	170.3
Germany, West	3,884	1,997	2,026	80.8	93.8	93.7	2,211	2,718	2,756	187.3	189.9
Italy	1,003	882	801	36.1	43.4	80	525	556	418	38.3	28.9
Luxembourg	39	35	---	65.9	88.6	---	37	45	---	3.1	---
Netherlands	282	217	188	103.8	115.9	113.6	425	365	310	25.1	21.6
Total EEC	6,781	5,889	5,588	63.4	79.6	77.5	6,236	6,803	6,283	468.7	432.9
Austria	376	306	294	61.5	75.6	67.7	336	336	289	23.1	19.9
Denmark	472	600	531	101.2	103.9	110.3	693	905	850	62.3	58.6
Finland	1,153	1,124	---	65	57.7	---	846	940	---	64.9	---
Greece	311	281	258	33.1	40.4	28.8	150	165	108	11.4	7.4
Ireland	352	238	230	71.6	82.5	80.6	366	285	269	19.6	18.5
Norway	136	111	106	70.4	76.3	70.2	139	123	108	8.3	7.4
Portugal	689	640	563	7.9	13.0	19.4	79	121	159	8.3	11.0
Spain	1,347	1,198	1,265	23.5	28.1	29.5	459	488	542	33.6	37.3
Sweden	1,240	1,124	1,147	85.6	85.6	82.9	1,272	1,396	1,381	96.2	95.1
Switzerland	33	22	---	89.8	97.1	---	43	31	---	2.1	---
United Kingdom	1,529	1,012	957	76.8	94.6	91.4	1,705	1,390	1,270	95.8	87.5
Total Western Europe 6/	14,420	12,545	12,090	58.9	71.3	69.7	12,325	12,985	12,230	894.6	842.6

		Area		Yield per acre			Production			
Bulgaria	373	321	30.3	38.6		164	180	--	12.4	--
Czechoslovakia	1,097	1,075	54.6	62.0		870	968	--	66.6	--
Germany, East	835	667	74.3	87.3		900	845	--	58.2	--
Hungary	245	138	34.8	30.9		124	62	--	4.3	--
Poland	3,988	3,529	46.6	54.7		2,700	2,800	--	192.9	--
Romania	447	309	28.7	37.9		186	170	--	11.7	--
Yugoslavia	801	744	30.1	33.6		350	363	--	25.0	--
Total Eastern Europe 6/	7,790	6,785	46.8	54.7	53.9	5,295	5,390	5,220	371.3	359.6
Total Europe 6/	22,210	19,330	54.6	65.5	63.7	17,620	18,375	17,450	1,255.9	1,202.2
U.S.S.R. (Europe and Asia) 2/	21,050	21,500	21.5	30.8	--	6,560	9,600	--	661.4	--
Africa:										
Morocco	58	35	20.2	21.7	35.1	17	11	25	0.8	1.7
South Africa, Republic of	509	745	15.6	17.0	--	115	184	--	12.7	--
Total 6/	710	860	16.0	17.2	--	165	215	--	14.8	--
Asia:										
Turkey	1,019	964	31.3	33.4	31.4	463	475	440	32.7	30.3
Japan	192	59	54.3	61.6	59.8	151	101	86	7.0	5.9
Total 6/	4,850	4,490	21.3	21.2	20.6	1,500	1,390	1,340	95.8	92.3
Oceania:										
Australia	3,383	3,020	25.0	16.3	--	1,228	714	--	49.2	--
New Zealand	33	22	85.9	78.8	--	41	25	--	1.7	--
Total 6/	3,416	3,042	25.6	16.7	--	1,269	739	--	50.9	--
World Total 6/	86,330	74,460 / 77,180	38.8	43.8	45.0	48,655	47,300	50,370	3,258.7	3,470.2

1/ Years shown refer to years of harvest in the Northern Hemisphere. Harvests of Northern Hemisphere countries are combined with those of the Southern Hemisphere which immediately follow; thus, the crop harvested in the Northern Hemisphere in 1968 is combined with preliminary forecasts for the Southern Hemisphere harvests which begin late in 1968 and end early in 1969. 2/ Harvested area as far as possible. 3/ Yield per acre calculated from acreage and production data shown. 4/ Preliminary estimates for Northern Hemisphere countries; for Southern Hemisphere, preliminary forecasts based largely on acreage and weather conditions to date. 5/ Production and yield reported in bushels of 34 pounds. 6/ Estimated totals include allowances for any missing data for countries shown and for other producing countries not shown. 7/ Production estimated.

Foreign Agricultural Service. Prepared or estimated on the basis of official statistics of foreign governments, other foreign source materials, reports of U.S. Agricultural Attaches and Foreign Service Officers, results of office research and related information.

BARLEY: Acreage, yield per acre, and production in specified countries, year of harvest, average 1960-64, annual 1967 and 1968 1/

Continent and country	Acreage 2/ Average 1960-64 (1,000 acres)	Acreage 1967 (1,000 acres)	Acreage 1968 4/ (1,000 acres)	Yield per acre 3/ Average 1960-64 (Bushels)	Yield 1967 (Bushels)	Yield 1968 4/ (Bushels)	Production Average 1960-64 (1,000 m.t.)	Production 1967 (1,000 m.t.)	Production 1968 4/ (1,000 m.t.)	Production Average 1960-64 (Million bushels)	Production 1967 (Million bushels)	Production 1968 4/ (Million bushels)
North America:												
Canada	5,866	8,115	8,836	28.4	30.6	36.8	3,752	5,414	6,884	172.3	248.7	316.2
United States	12,078	9,188	9,999	33.8	40.3	42.5	8,831	8,061	9,244	405.6	370.2	424.6
Mexico	572	554	556	13.5	14.5	14.9	169	175	180	7.8	8.0	8.3
Total 5/	18,520	17,860	19,395	31.6	35.1	38.6	12,755	13,655	16,310	585.9	627.2	749.1
South America:												
Argentina	1,517	1,226	—	22.8	22.0	—	753	588	—	34.6	27.0	—
Brazil	169	178	—	33.2	22.6	—	122	165	—	5.6	7.6	—
Colombia	140	151	151	35.8	28.6	35.0	109	94	115	5.0	4.3	5.3
Ecuador	265	264	264	14.9	18.3	18.3	86	105	105	3.9	4.8	4.8
Peru	449	432	—	19.0	19.1	—	186	180	170	8.5	8.3	7.8
Uruguay	120	74	—	13.1	8.7	—	34	14	—	1.6	0.6	—
Total 5/	2,650	2,330	2,350	22.4	22.7	23.8	1,295	1,150	—	59.5	52.8	52.8
Europe:												
EEC:												
Belgium	305	381	385	68.9	75.1	68.6	458	623	575	21.0	28.6	26.4
France	5,645	6,820	6,724	50.8	65.5	60.7	6,239	9,724	8,890	286.5	446.6	408.3
Germany, West	2,735	3,232	3,281	57.6	67.3	68.8	3,433	4,734	4,915	157.7	217.4	225.7
Italy	517	447	432	23.6	30.0	27.3	266	295	257	12.2	13.5	11.8
Luxembourg	20	32	—	46.2	66.0	—	20	46	—	0.9	2.1	—
Netherlands	227	264	263	75.7	77.8	76.8	374	447	440	17.2	20.5	20.2
Total EEC	9,449	11,176	11,115	52.4	65.2	62.5	10,790	15,869	15,117	495.6	728.8	694.3
Austria	517	573	588	51.2	61.9	53.0	576	772	679	26.5	35.5	31.2
Denmark	2,112	2,856	3,076	70.5	70.5	75.6	3,241	4,385	5,062	148.9	201.4	232.5
Finland	560	855	866	31.8	36.6	26.0	387	681	490	17.8	31.3	22.5
Greece	456	966	866	25.0	39.9	26.0	248	839	610	11.4	38.5	28.0
Ireland	396	451	447	58.2	63.0	62.7	502	629	629	23.1	28.9	28.9
Norway	407	442	442	47.7	50.5	47.8	423	486	460	19.4	22.3	21.1
Portugal	305	331	353	8.5	12.2	14.4	56	88	111	2.6	4.0	5.1
Spain	3,536	3,707	5,058	24.6	32.6	32.1	1,893	2,632	3,535	86.9	120.9	162.4
Sweden	933	1,310	1,364	51.6	54.8	54.9	1,049	1,564	1,631	48.2	71.8	74.9
Switzerland	75	77	—	60.3	88.3	—	99	148	148	4.5	6.8	6.8
United Kingdom	4,186	6,027	5,945	64.6	71.6	67.9	5,891	9,390	8,788	270.6	431.3	403.6
Total Western Europe 5/	22,935	28,770	30,190	50.4	59.8	56.7	25,155	37,485	37,300	1,155.4	1,721.7	1,713.2
Bulgaria	793	1,038	—	37.2	43.6	—	643	986	—	29.5	45.3	—
Czechoslovakia	1,717	1,749	—	43.5	50.8	—	1,625	1,936	—	74.6	88.9	—
Germany, East	1,029	1,366	—	54.2	64.8	—	1,214	1,927	—	55.8	88.5	—
Hungary	1,278	1,104	—	34.5	38.6	—	960	927	—	44.1	42.6	—
Poland	1,754	1,614	—	35.1	39.8	—	1,342	1,400	—	61.6	64.3	—
Romania	603	618	—	30.3	40.1	—	398	540	—	18.3	24.8	—
Yugoslavia	892	848	—	27.1	32.8	—	527	606	—	24.2	27.8	—
Total Eastern Europe 5/	8,070	8,340	8,320	38.2	45.8	42.2	6,710	8,325	7,650	308.2	382.4	351.4
Total Europe 5/	31,005	37,110	38,510	47.2	56.7	53.6	31,865	45,810	44,950	1,463.5	2,104.0	2,064.6
U.S.S.R. (Europe and Asia) 6/	41,513	47,196	—	17.8	20.1	—	16,117	20,700	—	740.3	950.7	—

- 4 -

Africa:												
Algeria	2,254	—	—	11.6	—	569	—	—	50.5	—	—
Morocco	4,254	4,465	4,685	11.9	11.3	1,104	1,100	2,224	46.8	—	102.1
Tunisia	1,310	—	—	4.8	—	138	80	130	32.2	3.7	6.0
United Arab Republic	133	125	—	49.0	40.4	142	110	—	2.1	5.1	—
South Africa, Republic of	84	121	—	19.7	15.6	36	41	—	13.8	1.9	—
Total 5/	10,385	9,515	10,180	11.5	11.8	2,590	2,455	3,725	112.8	—	171.1
Asia:												
Cyprus	161	198	—	19.1	19.9	67	86	40	4.0	1.8	
Iran	3,500	3,650	4,423	12.5	12.8	13.2	950	1,020	1,270	46.8	58.3
Iraq	2,695	—	—	15.3	—	897	700	—	32.2	—	
Israel	165	104	—	18.0	19.9	65	45	—	2.1	—	
Syria	1,859	—	—	13.4	—	542	300	—	13.8	—	
Turkey	6,816	6,733	6,672	22.3	25.9	23.4	3,310	3,800	3,400	174.5	156.2
Afghanistan	862	—	—	16.1	—	378	—	—	—	—	
India	7,765	7,065	7,423	15.6	15.9	21.6	2,630	2,449	3,500	112.5	160.8
Japan	1,575	872	781	.465	54.4	60.0	1,593	1,032	1,020	47.4	46.8
Korea, South	2,500	2,400	2,417	29.1	36.4	39.6	1,332	1,916	2,084	88.0	95.7
Pakistan 6/	541	456	490	11.6	11.6	11.6	136	106	124	4.8	5.7
Total 5/	46,190	42,400	43,270	18.6	19.9	20.3	18,710	18,380	19,130	844.2	878.6
Oceania:												
Australia	2,263	2,489	2,945	22.4	14.9	1,065	805	—	37.0	—	
New Zealand	82	100	—	54.8	67.7	98	147	—	6.8	—	
Total 5/	2,345	2,589	3,045	22.8	16.9	1,163	952	—	43.7	—	
World Total 5/ ..	152,620	159,000	163,450	25.4	29.8	30.1	84,495	103,100	107,250	4,735.3	4,925.9

1/ Years shown refer to years of harvest in the Northern Hemisphere. Harvests of Northern Hemisphere countries are combined with those of Southern Hemisphere which immediately follow; thus, the crop harvested in the Northern Hemisphere in 1968 is combined with preliminary forecasts for Southern Hemisphere harvests which begin late in 1968 and end early in 1969. 2/ Harvested area as far as known. 3/ Yield per acre calculated from acreage and production data. 4/ Preliminary estimates for Northern Hemisphere countries; for Southern Hemisphere, preliminary forecasts based largely on acreage and weather conditions to date. 5/ Estimated totals include allowances for producing countries not shown. 6/ Production estimated.

Foreign Agricultural Service. Prepared on the basis of official statistics for foreign governments, other foreign materials, reports of U.S. Agricultural Attachés and Foreign Service Officers, results of office research, and related information.

The East European barley crop is estimated at 7.7 million tons, 9 percent below the 1967 harvest but similar to that of 1966. Poland, East Germany, and Czechoslovakia had good crops. However, drought sharply reduced yields in Hungary, Romania, Yugoslavia, and Bulgaria. Barley production in the Soviet Union is currently estimated slightly lower than in 1967.

The African barley crop was up sharply, mainly because of a big harvest in Morocco. Unusually good rains doubled the crop there as compared with last year.

Barley production in Asia is estimated at 19.1 million tons, up 4 percent. While production declined in Turkey, it was substantially higher than in Iran, India, and South Korea.

The barley crop in South America is expected to be about the same as in 1967. However, Australia is expected to have a record harvest, a result of exceptionally good moisture supplies during the season.

World oat production in 1968 is estimated at 50.4 million tons, 6 percent over 1967 and the highest since 1960. World acreage and yield are estimated higher by 4 percent and 3 percent, respectively.

The North American oat crop, at 19.1 million tons, was up 19 percent. Canada increased production by 18 percent, mostly on increased yield. The U.S. oat crop, at 13.6 million tons, was 20 percent over last year. Area gained 11 percent to 17.8 million acres, and yield rose 7 percent to a record 52.6 bushels per acre.

Oat production in Europe is estimated at 17.4 million tons, 5 percent below last year's high. The West European crop, at 12.2 million tons, was down 6 percent, as area declined 4 percent to a new low. Oat production in the Common Market countries, at 6.3 million tons, declined 8 percent. The West German crop, at 2.8 million tons, gained slightly. However, yields declined in most countries of the area. The French harvest was down 10 percent on an 8-percent reduction in area, and that in the United Kingdom was 9 percent lower as acreage declined 5 percent.

The East European oat harvest is estimated 3 percent lower, at 5.2 million tons. The northern, heavy producing countries of that region had crops similar to those of a year ago.

Oat production in the Soviet Union is estimated close to the 1967 crop. Little change is estimated in the African and Asian oat harvests.

In South America the Argentine crop should about equal that of 1967, but drought in Chile could cause the total for the continent to be below that of the previous year. Favored with good weather, Australia should have a near-record oat harvest.

UNITED STATES DEPARTMENT OF AGRICULTURE

WASHINGTON, D. C.   20250

Official Business

NOTICE

If you no longer need this publication,
check here ☐ return this sheet,
and your name will be dropped from
the mailing list.

If your address should be changed ☐
PRINT or TYPE the new address,
including ZIP CODE, and return the
whole sheet to:

Foreign Agricultural Service, Rm. 5918
U. S. Department of Agriculture
Washington, D. C. 20250

GRAIN
FG 13-68
December 1968

WORLD CORN PRODUCTION

SECOND OF RECORD IN 1968

World corn production in 1968 is estimated at 234 million metric tons, 2 percent below the 1967 record crop of 239 million tons, on the basis of information available to the Foreign Agricultural Service. World corn area, at 254 million acres, was virtually unchanged.

Corn production in North America is estimated at 125.8 million tons, down 5 percent on 4 percent less acreage. The Canadian crop is placed at about 2.0 million tons, up 5 percent on 9 percent larger area.

Corn production in the United States is reported at 112.8 million tons, 6 percent below the record 1967 crop. U.S. acreage declined 7 percent to 55.9 million; yield gained slightly to a new high of 79.4 million bushels per acre. Growing conditions were very favorable in the Corn Belt States; however, heavy rains and high winds in October reduced yields from earlier expectations.

Mexican corn production is estimated at 9.0 million tons, up 6 percent on larger area and improved yields.

The European corn crop is estimated at 29.6 million tons, 2 percent below 1967. The West European harvest, however, gained 16 percent, to 11.8 million tons, as growing conditions were favorable in most areas. French corn production was 33 percent over last year's drought-reduced crop, at a record 4.9 million tons. French yield was at a new high of 77.1 bushels per acre. Italian production at 4.0 million tons was up 4 percent. The EEC corn harvest totaled 9.2 million tons, up 19 percent with a 3 percent gain in area and a 15 percent increase in yield. Spanish production gained for the third successive year, to a record 1.5 million tons, up 20 percent.

CORN: Acreage, yield per acre, and production in specified countries, year of harvest, average 1960-64, annual 1967-68 1/

Continent and country	Acreage			Yield per acre 3/			Production				
	Average 1960-64 (1,000 acres)	1967 (1,000 acres)	1968 4/ (1,000 acres)	Average 1960-64 (Bushels)	1967 (Bushels)	1968 4/ (Bushels)	Average 1960-64 (1,000 m.t.)	1967 (1,000 m.t.)	1968 4/ (1,000 m.t.)	1967 (Million bushels)	1968 4/ (Million bushels)
North America:											
Canada	500	876	956	71.0	84.6	81.7	903	832	1,984	74.1	78.1
United States	59,876	60,385	55,886	62.5	78.2	79.4	94,562	119,943	112,70	4,722.2	4,439.8
Costa Rica	175	180	180	16.9	17.1	18.6	76	78	85	3.1	3.3
El Salvador	448	450	---	17.2	17.7	---	196	202	250	8.0	9.8
Guatemala	1,682	847	---	13.3	15.0	---	570	690	727	27.2	28.6
Honduras	959	1,013	---	12.5	13.8	---	303	355	390	14.0	15.4
Mexico	15,416	18,740	19,274	15.5	13.8	18.4	6,064	8,500	9,00	334.6	354.3
Nicaragua	353	500	---	13.9	13.7	---	124	174	180	6.8	7.1
Panama	213	279	---	13.3	12.6	---	72	89	96	3.3	3.5
Total 5/	80,640	85,250	81,450	50.4	61.0	60.8	103,220	132,210	125,760	5,204.8	4,950.9
South America:											
Argentina	7,008	8,508	---	28.0	30.3	---	4,984	6,560	---	258.3	---
Brazil	19,308	22,980	---	20.6	21.3	---	10,112	12,452	---	490.2	---
Chile	183	217	215	37.9	55.2	48.3	176	304	264	12.0	10.4
Colombia	874	1,952	1,915	17.5	17.1	17.4	807	850	845	33.5	33.3
Ecuador	508	524	519	11.7	14.0	13.7	151	185	180	7.3	7.1
Peru	833	890	---	23.2	24.8	---	490	560	---	22.0	---
Uruguay	563	400	---	10.3	6.8	---	147	69	---	2.7	---
Venezuela	1,058	1,208	---	17.2	19.7	---	461	604	---	23.8	---
Total 5/	32,290	37,780	---	21.7	23.0	---	17,820	22,100	---	870.0	---
Europe:											
EEC:											
France	2,229	2,525	2,501	46.4	57.4	77.1	2,625	3,679	4,900	144.8	192.9
Germany, West	41	104	156	37.6	74.2	71.2	39	196	282	7.7	11.1
Italy	2,816	2,513	2,639	52.2	60.5	59.7	3,732	3,860	4,000	152.0	157.5
Total EEC	5,086	5,142	5,296	49.5	59.2	68.2	6,396	7,735	9,182	304.5	361.5
Austria	130	148	183	61.2	85.0	75.9	202	316	353	12.4	13.9
Greece	461	344	---	24.4	38.7	---	286	338	---	13.3	---
Portugal	1,208	1,161	1,137	18.3	19.3	19.3	562	570	558	22.4	22.0
Spain	1,139	1,203	1,295	37.2	40.1	44.7	1,075	1,224	1,470	48.2	57.9
Total Western Europe 2/	8,030	8,000	8,225	41.8	50.1	56.6	8,520	10,185	11,830	401.0	465.7
Bulgaria	1,601	1,404	---	40.7	57.7	---	1,655	2,058	---	81.0	---
Czechoslovakia	509	361	---	39.7	46.1	---	509	423	---	16.7	---
Hungary	3,226	3,054	---	40.3	45.4	---	3,304	3,522	---	138.7	---
Romania	8,305	7,959	---	27.4	33.9	---	5,784	6,858	---	270.0	---
Yugoslavia 5/	6,118	6,202	6,054	36.4	45.7	42.3	5,664	7,200	6,500	283.5	255.9
Total Eastern Europe 5/	19,760	18,980	18,695	33.7	41.6	37.4	16,920	20,065	17,740	789.9	698.4
Total Europe 5/	27,790	26,980	26,920	36.0	44.1	43.2	25,440	30,250	29,570	1,190.9	1,164.1

U.S.S.R. (Europe and Asia) 6/	15,518	8,611	---	24.3	36.6	---	9,564	8,000	---	314.9	---
Africa:											
Morocco	1,122	1,139	1,118	11.4	8.6	8.5	297	250	240	9.8	9.4
United Arab Republic	1,793	1,682	---	40.0	53.8	---	1,823	2,300	---	90.5	---
Angola	1,465	---	---	10.9	---	---	407	---	---	---	---
Kenya	2,900	3,100	3,000	18.5	20.7	20.2	1,360	1,633	1,542	64.3	60.7
Malagasy Republic	247	---	---	14.4	---	---	90	---	---	---	---
South Africa, Republic of	13,106	---	---	15.5	---	---	5,147	5,316	---	209.3	---
Total 5/	35,700	35,900	---	17.1	18.9	---	15,500	17,250	---	679.1	---
Asia:											
Turkey	1,689	1,668	1,66	21.4	25.5	23.8	916	1,080	1,000	42.5	39.4
China, Mainland	---	---	---	---	---	---	11,580	---	---	---	---
Afghanistan	1,236	---	---	22.5	---	---	707	---	---	---	---
China, Taiwan	43	59	---	29.4	42.7	---	32	64	---	2.5	---
India	11,200	13,141	---	15.5	18.8	---	4,402	6,275	6,500	247.0	255.9
Indonesia	7,96	7,413	---	15.5	15.7	---	2,823	2,90	---	116.5	---
Japan	00	52	44	40.9	46.2	44.7	104	61	50	2.4	2.0
Pakistan	1,190	5,1	1,550	16.5	20.7	---	498	795	1,555	31.3	61.2
Philippines	4,759	5,572	5,609	10.2	10.7	10.9	1,230	1,517	1,300	59.7	51.2
Thailand	922	---	---	30.7	---	---	720	1,200	---	47.2	---
Total 5/	53,400	58,900	59,300	17.2	19.1	18.8	23,390	28,590	28,340	1,125.5	1,115.7
Oceania:											
Australia	206	209	205	33.6	35.9	37.1	176	190	193	7.5	7.6
New Zealand	8	8	---	77.8	91.5	---	16	19	---	.7	---
Total 5/	214	217	---	35.3	37.8	---	192	209	---	8.2	---
World Total 5/	245,550	253,640	254,420	31.3	37.0	36.2	195,130	238,610	233,910	9,394.0	9,209.0

1/ Years shown refer to years of harvest in the Northern Hemisphere. Harvests of Northern Hemisphere countries are combined with those of the Southern Hemisphere which immediately follow; thus, the crop harvested in the Northern Hemisphere in 1968 is combined with preliminary forecasts for the Southern Hemisphere harvest which begins in late in 1968 and ends early in 1969. 2/ Harvested area as far as possible. 3/ Yield per acre calculated from acreage and production data shown. 4/ Preliminary estimates for Northern Hemisphere countries; for the Southern Hemisphere, preliminary forecasts. 5/ Estimated totals include allowances for producing countries not shown. 6/ Production estimated.

Foreign Agricultural Service. Prepared or estimated on the basis of official statistics of foreign governments, other foreign source materials, reports of U.S. Agricultural Attaches and Foreign Service Officers, results of office research and related information.

- 4 -

The East European corn crop is estimated at 17.7 million tons, 12 percent
below last year and 21 percent below the 1966 total. Drought, more serious
than last year, in the principal corn producing countries of the area was
responsible for the sharply reduced outturn. Yugoslavia's corn harvest is
estimated at 6.5 million tons, down 10 percent.

Corn acreage and production in the Soviet Union are currently expected to
be moderately larger than last year.

The Asian corn harvest is estimated at 28.3 million tons, about the same
as 1967.

The Australian crop is placed up slightly at 193,000 tons. Corn outturn
in Africa will depend largely on South African recovery from the previous
poor crop.

It is too early to estimate performance in South America; however, the
Argentine corn acreage is expected to be somewhat larger, which should
result in a larger crop to be harvested there next spring.

GRAIN
FG 13-68
December 1968

WORLD CORN PRODUCTION

SECOND OF RECORD IN 1968

World corn production in 1968 is estimated at 234 million metric tons, 2 percent below the 1967 record crop of 239 million tons, on the basis of information available to the Foreign Agricultural Service. World corn area, at 254 million acres, was virtually unchanged.

Corn production in North America is estimated at 125.8 million tons, down 5 percent on 4 percent less acreage. The Canadian crop is placed at about 2.0 million tons, up 5 percent on 9 percent larger area.

Corn production in the United States is reported at 112.8 million tons, 6 percent below the record 1967 crop. U.S. acreage declined 7 percent to 55.9 million; yield gained slightly to a new high of 79.4 million bushels per acre. Growing conditions were very favorable in the Corn Belt States; however, heavy rains and high winds in October reduced yields from earlier expectations.

Mexican corn production is estimated at 9.0 million tons, up 6 percent on larger area and improved yields.

The European corn crop is estimated at 29.6 million tons, 2 percent below 1967. The West European harvest, however, gained 16 percent, to 11.8 million tons, as growing conditions were favorable in most areas. French corn production was 33 percent over last year's drought-reduced crop, at a record 4.9 million tons. French yield was at a new high of 77.1 bushels per acre. Italian production at 4.0 million tons was up 4 percent. The EEC corn harvest totaled 9.2 million tons, up 19 percent with a 3 percent gain in area and a 15 percent increase in yield. Spanish production gained for the third successive year, to a record 1.5 million tons, up 20 percent.

CORN: Acreage, yield per acre, and production in specified countries, year of harvest, average 1960-64, annual 1967-68 1/

Continent and country	Acreage 2/			Yield per acre 3/			Production				
	Average 1960-64 (1,000 acres)	1967 (1,000 acres)	1968 4/ (1,000 acres)	Average 1960-64 (Bushels)	1967 (Bushels)	1968 4/ (Bushels)	Average 1960-64 (1,000 m.t.)	1967 (1,000 m.t.)	1968 4/ (1,000 m.t.)	1967 (Million bushels)	1968 4/ (Million bushels)
North America:											
Canada	500	876	956	71.0	84.6	81.7	903	1,882	1,984	74.1	78.1
United States	59,876	60,385	55,886	62.5	78.2	79.4	94,562	119,943	112,770	4,722.2	4,439.8
Costa Rica	175	180	180	16.9	17.1	18.6	76	78	85	3.1	3.3
El Salvador	448	450	---	17.2	17.7	---	196	202	250	8.0	9.8
Guatemala	1,682	1,847	---	13.3	15.0	---	570	690	727	27.2	28.6
Honduras	959	1,013	---	12.5	13.8	---	303	355	390	14.0	15.4
Mexico	15,416	18,740	19,274	15.5	17.9	18.4	6,064	8,500	9, 00	334.6	354.3
Nicaragua	353	500	---	13.9	13.7	---	124	174	180	6.8	7.1
Panama	213	279	---	13.6	12.6	---	72	89	96	3.3	3.5
Total 5/	80,640	85,250	81,450	50.4	61.0	60.8	103,220	132,210	125,760	5,204.8	4,950.9
South America:											
Argentina	7,008	8,508	---	28.0	30.3	---	4,984	6,560	---	258.3	---
Brazil	19,308	22,980	---	20.6	21.3	---	10,112	12,452	---	490.2	---
Chile	183	217	215	37.9	55.2	48.3	176	304	264	12.0	10.4
Colombia	1,814	1,952	1,915	17.5	17.1	17.4	807	850	845	33.5	33.3
Ecuador	508	524	519	11.7	14.0	13.7	151	185	180	7.3	7.1
Peru	833	890	---	23.2	24.8	---	490	560	---	22.0	---
Uruguay	563	400	---	10.3	6.8	---	147	69	---	2.7	---
Venezuela	1,058	1,208	---	17.2	19.7	---	461	604	---	23.8	---
Total 5/	32,290	37,780	---	21.7	23.0	---	17,820	22,100	---	870.0	---
Europe:											
EEC:											
France	2,229	2,525	2,501	46.4	57.4	77.1	2,625	3,679	4,900	144.8	192.9
Germany, West	41	104	156	37.6	74.2	71.2	39	196	282	7.7	11.1
Italy	2,816	2,513	2,639	52.2	60.5	59.7	3,732	3,860	4,000	152.0	157.5
Total EEC	5,086	5,142	5,296	49.5	59.2	68.2	6,396	7,735	9,182	304.5	361.5
Austria	130	148	183	61.2	85.0	75.9	202	316	353	12.4	13.9
Greece	461	344	---	24.4	38.7	---	286	338	---	13.3	---
Portugal	1,208	1,161	1,137	18.3	19.3	19.3	562	570	558	22.4	22.0
Spain	1,139	1,203	1,295	37.2	40.1	44.7	1,075	1,224	1,470	48.2	57.9
Total Western Europe 5/	8,030	8,000	8,225	41.8	50.1	56.6	8,520	10,185	11,830	401.0	465.7
Bulgaria	1,601	1,404	---	40.7	57.7	---	1,655	2,058	---	81.0	---
Czechoslovakia	509	361	---	39.7	46.1	---	509	423	---	16.7	---
Hungary	3,226	3,054	---	40.3	45.4	---	3,304	3,522	---	138.7	---
Romania	8,305	7,959	---	27.4	33.9	---	5,784	6,858	---	270.0	---
Yugoslavia 5/	6,118	6,202	6,054	36.4	45.7	42.3	5,664	7,200	6,500	283.5	255.9
Total Eastern Europe 5/	19,760	18,980	18,695	33.7	41.6	37.4	16,920	20,065	17,760	789.9	698.4
Total Europe 5/	27,790	26,980	26,920	36.0	44.1	43.2	25,440	30,250	29,570	1,190.9	1,164.1

U.S.S.R. (Europe and Asia) 6/	15,518	8,611	--	24.3	36.6	--	9,564	8,000	--	314.9	--
Africa:											
Morocco	1,122	1,139	1,118	11.4	8.6	8.5	297	250	240	9.8	9.4
United Arab Republic	798	1,682	--	40.0	53.8	--	1,823	2,300	--	90.5	--
Angola	1,465	--	--	10.9	--	--	407	--	--	--	--
Kenya	2,900	3,100	3,000	18.5	20.7	20.2	1,360	1,623	1,542	64.3	60.7
Malagasy Republic	247	--	--	14.4	--	--	90	--	--	--	--
South Africa, Republic of	13,106	--	--	15.5	--	--	5,147	5,316	--	209.3	--
Total 5/	35,700	35,900	--	17.1	18.9	--	15,500	17,250	--	679.1	--
Asia:											
Turkey	1,689	1,668	1,656	21.4	25.5	23.8	916	1,080	1,000	42.5	39.4
China, Mainland	--	--	--	--	--	--	11,580	--	--	--	--
Afghanistan	1,236	--	--	22.5	--	--	707	--	--	--	--
China, Taiwan	43	59	--	29.4	42.7	--	32	64	--	2.5	--
India	11,200	13,141	--	15.5	18.8	--	4,402	6,275	6,500	247.6	255.9
Indonesia	7,156	7,413	--	15.5	15.7	--	2,823	2,960	--	116.5	--
Japan	100	52	44	40.9	46.2	44.7	104	61	50	2.4	2.0
Pakistan	1,190	1,511	1,550	16.5	20.7	--	498	795	--	31.7	--
Philippines	4,759	5,572	5,609	10.2	10.7	10.9	1,230	1,517	1,555	59.2	61.2
Thailand	922	--	--	30.7	--	--	720	1,200	1,300	47.2	51.2
Total 5/	53,400	58,900	59,300	17.2	19.1	18.8	23,390	28,590	28,340	1,125.5	1,115.7
Oceania:											
Australia	206	209	205	33.6	35.9	37.1	176	190	193	7.5	7.6
New Zealand	8	8	--	77.8	91.5	--	16	19	--	.7	--
Total 5/	214	217	--	35.3	37.8	--	192	209	--	8.2	--
World Total 5/	245,550	253,640	254,420	31.3	37.0	36.2	195,130	238,610	233,910	9,394.0	9,209.0

1/ Years shown refer to years of harvest in the Northern Hemisphere. Harvests of Northern Hemisphere countries are combined with those of the Southern Hemisphere which immediately follow; thus, the crop harvested in the Northern Hemisphere in 1968 is combined with preliminary forecasts for the Southern Hemisphere harvest which begins in late in 1968 and ends early in 1969. 2/ Harvested area as far as possible. 3/ Yield per acre calculated from acreage and production data shown. 4/ Preliminary estimates for Northern Hemisphere countries; for the Southern Hemisphere, preliminary forecasts. 5/ Estimated totals include allowances for producing countries not shown. 6/ Production estimated.

Foreign Agricultural Service. Prepared or estimated on the basis of official statistics of foreign governments, other foreign source materials, reports of U.S. Agricultural Attaches and Foreign Service Officers, results of office research and related information.

- 4 -

The East European corn crop is estimated at 17.7 million tons, 12 percent
below last year and 21 percent below the 1966 total. Drought, more serious
than last year, in the principal corn producing countries of the area was
responsible for the sharply reduced outturn. Yugoslavia's corn harvest is
estimated at 6.5 million tons, down 10 percent.

Corn acreage and production in the Soviet Union are currently expected to
be moderately larger than last year.

The Asian corn harvest is estimated at 28.3 million tons, about the same
as 1967.

The Australian crop is placed up slightly at 193,000 tons. Corn outturn
in Africa will depend largely on South African recovery from the previous
poor crop.

It is too early to estimate performance in South America; however, the
Argentine corn acreage is expected to be somewhat larger, which should
result in a larger crop to be harvested there next spring.

CPSIA information can be obtained
at www.ICGtesting.com
Printed in the USA
BVHW040824110219
539952BV00005B/76/P

9 780260 520166